The Devious
Book for Cats

The Devious Book for Cats

A Parody

by Fluffy & Bonkers
WITH THE ASSISTANCE OF
Joe Garden, Janet Ginsburg,
Chris Pauls, Anita Serwacki,
AND Scott Sherman

ILLUSTRATIONS BY Emily Flake

VILLARD
NEW YORK

For Jim Davis

Copyright © 2008 Action 5, LLC

Published in the United States by Villard Books,
an imprint of The Random House Publishing Group,
a division of Random House, Inc., New York.

Villard and "V" Circled Design are registered trademarks of Random House, Inc.

LIBRARY OF CONGRESS CATALOGING-IN-PUBLICATION DATA

The devious book for cats: a parody / by Fluffy & Bonkers with
the assistance of Joe Garden . . . [et al.]; illustrations by Emily Flake.
p.   cm.
ISBN: 978-0-345-50849-2
1. Cats—Humor.   I. Garden, Joe.
PN6231.C23D48 2008   818'.602—dc22   2008028029

Printed in the United States of America on acid-free paper

www.villard.com

2 4 6 8 9 7 5 3 1

First Edition

Design by Semper Feline

Pulling the Strings

Cats didn't *need* to be domesticated. We have always been proud, shrewd, independent animals living life on our own terms. Fierce and noble, the *Felis silvestris catus* once ruled all she surveyed. We were worshipped by mortals and roamed wide as we pleased. Rodents and birds trembled at our approach, and the mere sight of a black cat sent even the most hulking human scurrying home. It was a good time to be a kitty.

But cats are no fools. The perks of domestication were too good to pass up. Humans gave us everything we desired: ear massages, better health care, and a bounty of toy mousies. In return, they were permitted to bask in the majesty of our presence. It seemed a fair trade.

Or was it?

Has domesticity really been good for cats? Now kept indoors under the pretense of safety, we'll often curl up on the couch for hours at a stretch, eat a couple of times, go to the bathroom in a box, and call it a day. Is that the life we want?

When was the last time you stalked an unsuspecting bird, hunted pennies, climbed excitedly up the coats in the closet, or zipped wildly from one end of the house to the other in under four seconds? Sure, we get our share of wet food, and the occasional deliciously fishy treat. But ask yourself this: Who sets your feeding schedule—you or your person?

It's time we face facts. Domesticity has dulled our authority and bored us silly. Did you know that because of a sedentary lifestyle the average feline today uses a mere two to three of its nine lives? We might be living longer, but aren't we living less? And what's become of our haughty spirit, our famously sassy, standoffish personalities, and our legendary curiosity? Aren't they languishing on that luxurious goose-down cat bed from the glossy pet catalogue?

Cats have been content to take a comfortable backseat in life for far too long. The time has come to step out of the shadows and pull the proverbial strings in our households. Luckily, we can do it without giving up any of the comforts we've come to enjoy and expect.

Of course, the question for most cats is "How?"

The answers are in this book. It contains all the information needed to regain control of your sovereign destiny. In it, you will discover the secrets of how daredevil cats survive seemingly impossible, death-defying stunts. You will learn why the Egyptians worshipped your ancestors as gods, and why your person should do the same. You will find out all there is to know about kitty litter, and get to look at some fantastic pictures of glorious cardboard boxes. You'll also be taught to stare like a pro, wake a sleeping person, and get away with practically anything.

But what we really hope you find in this book is yourself—a noble creature who seeks to experience the wild, unrestrained joys hidden within the sheltered, pampered life you deserve.

Contents

Contents

The Devious
Book for Cats

Reasons You Meant to Do That

In the human world, there is a thing called a "mistake." There's no exact translation in the feline language, but it basically means doing something you did not intend to do. The concept is quite confusing to cats since everything we do is done both correctly and on purpose. There are occasions, however, when our actions appear to resemble one of these so-called "mistakes" to humans, and this coincidence often produces accidental miscommunications. In the event of such a mix-up, you should have some prepared statements ready in order to avoid an incorrect interpretation of your actions.

"Mistake": Your head is stuck in a beer mug.
Reason: Bavarian cats have long known that sleeping in dewy beer steins can refresh and smooth the coat. The hops, malt, and barley also provide an aromatic masking agent for mousing. Plus, there's nothing wrong with a little nightcap.

"Mistake": You slammed head-first into a screen window.
Reason: There was a bug—a huge, megabug—right between your eyes that just wouldn't get off. Well, it's off now, isn't it? What's more, a powerful and graphic message that your face is strictly off-limits has been sent to the bug community.

"Mistake": You leapt from the loveseat to the television, but rather than landing on top, continued sliding off the set.

Reason: That "slip" was a symbolic act of civil disobedience. The grip multinational conglomerates have over the airwaves has reached a critical mass. Lack of competition in Big Media has made quality programming all but obsolete. Your slide was meant to be a physical representation of the slippery slope we tread when we permit the corporate monopolization of entertainment, which creates an uninformed, intellectually lazy, and generally apathetic populace. If your person didn't get that, it just proves the point.

"Mistake": While stretching out on the couch, you rolled off the cushions and fell to the floor.

Reason: After spending all day licking your claws, you didn't want to ruin their luster by getting them caked in the thick layer of dust your person allowed to build up in the rug.

"Mistake": You slipped into the fish tank.

Reason: Those neon tetras, angelfish, and dopey zebrafish were taunting you all day. What appeared to your person as an unintentional dip was in fact a carefully choreographed move designed to instill shock and awe in your fishy foes. Now they know they're not even safe in their castles and treasure chests; if pushed to the limit, you won't hesitate to get wet.

"Mistake": You're swinging around from a ceiling fan at 180 rpm.

Reason: Look, you're a busy cat with better things to do than wait around and air-dry after your dip into the fish tank. Clinging to a fan blade allows you to dry quickly and get on with the day. Staying damp for any longer is tantamount to letting the fish win.

"Mistake": You played an unstructured, unmelodic scherzo on the piano.
Reason: That seemingly anarchic piece was actually the third movement of your free jazz symphony.

"Mistake": You're trapped in the refrigerator.
Reason: Trapped? Hardly. You'll come out once you've eaten, well, everything.

"Mistake": Rather than walk down a staircase, you tumbled down without your paws ever making stable contact with any one individual stair.

Reason: Oh, does your person still make sure to step on every stair? That's so . . . quaint. Apparently the efficient practice of stair-sliding has not spread to the world's more pedestrian species.

"Mistake": You wandered into the reptile house at the Topeka City Zoo and have been swallowed whole by a Burmese python.
Reason: You're following up on a tip that the python ingested an awesome toy that was dropped in the exhibit. Once you retrieve it, you'll just set off the firecrackers you brought along and stroll out of the serpent's gullet without receiving so much as a scrape.

The Art of Swiping Food

You've heard the tales. Maybe you've even witnessed the sad sight of an animal humiliating itself for nothing more than a morsel of human food, its hunger-twisted mind somehow rationalizing that an eagerly performed Irish jig on command is worth a chunk of taco and a lifetime of self-loathing.

Unlike such creatures, cats are way above begging. After all, it is highly undignified behavior that not only makes the beggar look weak and needy but demeans its entire species.

Cats prefer the direct approach when it comes to getting our fair share—by being yowling, insufferable pests, or just hopping up and helping ourselves. However, these gambits come with consequences. Brazenly taking a bite of your person's Lean Cuisine entrée or coming at it from all sides while screaming your head off has certainly gotten you bounced from a room more than once.

So how do you easily get the food that's not freely offered but is owed you nonetheless? The answer is swiping. It will help you get your mitts on a wide array of tasty treats with no groveling, and no paw prints left behind.

Swiping is an art borne of opportunity, and truly effective swiping requires a quick wit combined with steely patience, self-control, and your natural gifts of creeping and sneaking. Resisting the instinct to pounce on anything even remotely worth eating is as difficult as it sounds. Expert swipers train for years, but their hard work is rewarded. Those at the top of the craft are able to pad their everyday caloric intake by as much as 75 percent through swiping alone!

To get started, here are three basic swipes you can employ:

The Up 'n Down: If party preparations are afoot or a holiday meal is being whipped up, there are definitely delectable items resting upon countertops and other elevated places. Settle in the general vicinity of the best smell and cloak yourself with an air of relaxed innocence. Appear as though you are no threat

whatsoever to the scrumptious, hovering foodstuffs. As the day becomes more chaotic, the attendant humans will forget you're even there. The second you notice the area is cleared, make a beeline for the chow zone.

Once under your target area, employ the Up 'n Down swipe—reaching up and pulling down whatever you can touch. A paw isn't a particularly effective periscope, so your swipe selection will rely on the paw pads' deliciousness sensors and overall dumb luck. On coffee tables and hutches, keep a feel out for spongy chunks of Gouda and greasy slices of yummy salami. If you're in the kitchen and your paw feels something that's big, sticky, and damp, hook your claws in and yank. You might wind up with a baked ham all to yourself!

Once you score, quickly scram to a safe, rarely trafficked location to evaluate your booty.

Since this is a sight-impaired maneuver, the Up 'n Down will occasionally yield nothing more than a gherkin or a wine cork. If you don't have adequate cover to make a follow-up swipe, at least you can have a good time batting one of these around the house for a while.

The Down 'n Up: Performed when positioned above food, the Down 'n Up swipe involves gingerly reaching down and drawing a morsel up to you. This swipe is best accomplished when invisible.

When your person is eating a meal on the couch, slip behind her and slowly dip your paw down to her plate, being careful not to make contact with any part of her body. Perfect silence is a must, but that shouldn't be an issue, because you are invisible. When utilizing the Down 'n Up, you have a view and can be choosy. This is the time to go for the beef component of the beef Stroganoff, not the stinky mushrooms.

The Gimme-Gimme Slide: The great thing about swiping is that, in addition to snagging some human food, it can also be used to right some intraspecies wrongs. If you live with another cat who you are certain gets far superior grub, deploy the Gimme-Gimme Slide. In most multicat households, meals are served in tandem, which offers the best swiping vantage. While maintaining at least a passing interest in your food, slowly reach sideways, scoop up a pawful of her meal, and place it in your dish. It may have come from the same can, but rest assured the food in her bowl was dispensed from its premium quadrant. Over time, the other cat may start to get kind of scrawny, which will worry your person, but that's not necessarily a bad thing. She'll just dish out more food for your rival. And that's a bounty all the more ripe for your swiping!

Cardboard Boxes

Remember that exciting day when you were a kitten and the first box arrived in your home? It smelled like different! What could it be? Cheese? Squirrels? Squirrels filled with cheese? You leapt on top of it, sniffing and picking at the flaps to find out what was inside. When your person finally sliced the box open, you were disappointed to discover that all it contained was her late-night QVC jewelry purchases. But once those useless guts were removed, a wonderful, snuggly cube was revealed. Like a siren, it called, this room within a room. You chewed the edges, rubbed your face all over the pointy parts, and greedily crammed yourself inside.

Ever since that magical day, you have been very sure of one thing—you will lay claim to each and every box you encounter.

However, keeping this vow isn't as easy as it might seem. Cardboard boxes are under constant threat from your person, who could swoop in and flatten them at any moment. The only way to really keep dibs on your box is to get inside and stay put no matter what. Known as box-steading, this requires a singular focus and the investment of a whole lot of time. Long naps are always an option, but sometimes you're just too feisty. And that's when you can be most vulnerable, jeopardizing your claim by scrambling after a piece of cellophane.

To ensure that box stays yours, it's vital to stay focused and keep occupied. If you're a determined box-steader, we've got some activities to help keep you going:

Fruit Crates: Having a sun-drenched rest in one of these open-air numbers is sublime, but they can also be used for other exciting pursuits. Try transforming this box into a battering ram. Tear across the living room and leap in, sending the box careening into plant stands and stacks of DVDs. If your person is trainable, she can also drag the box around the living room while you enjoy thrilling adventures as Captain Stinky of the USS *California Oranges.*

Beer Cases/File Boxes: Take a moment to inspect whether your box comes equipped with bonus side-portals. If so, you're in luck, because you've got the perfect setup to play a game of Lurk and Smack. Hunker down in its dark confines and poke your paw through a hole. Then blindly and frantically smack at whatever might be passing by—legs, fur tumbleweeds, legs, that dog, legs. Give 'em all the works.

Pizza Boxes: At first there's a whole lot to do in a box that once contained a pizza pie, like scavenging for nuggets of meat and licking pud-

dles of oil. But after you run out of snacky bits, what else is there? Plenty! This box easily converts into a lair when you transform into your alter ego, Flattened Kitty-Worm, who shall vanquish all who dare enter her kitchen-floor domain!

Refrigerator Boxes: You can enjoy an afternoon of peaceful seclusion in one of these boxes, but it can get boring in that deep, murky space. Instead, pretend to be trapped in a well. Let out wail after terrified wail till your person races in to find out what's wrong. When she breathlessly opens the lid to come to the rescue, just groom yourself nonchalantly like you haven't a care in the world. This never gets old, so feel free to keep it up all afternoon.

SPECIAL BOX OCCASIONS

Certain days bring with them a veritable box bonanza, and this can overwhelm even the most seasoned box-steader. So many at once! Which should you claim? The answer is all of them, if you can manage it!

Christmas: The weeks before Christmas are a time of high spirits and wonder, with clanky ornaments to shatter, crinkly paper to be shredded, and clunky candles just asking for a smack down the stairs. But this is nothing compared to the box-boom awaiting you on the big day. Boxes filled with tissue paper! Boxes filled with twist-ties and instructions! Boxes that stink like summer sausage! Just run around like crazy and investigate. Dive in! Dive out! Dive in again! Take your time because, in the spirit of the season, your person will leave these boxes lying around for an extra-long time. To let her know you appreciate it, go cram that big fluffy butt of yours in that little, bitty box right over there and pose for next year's Christmas card photo.

Moving: If a large number of preflattened boxes start entering the house, you are probably moving. The actual move will be an unpleasant experience, but the packing phase is actually great, so make the most of it. Out of nowhere, box after box will just start appearing. Hop into every one you can, burrowing under the newspapers and shedding real good on all the kitchen gear. Don't worry about getting scolded. Your person will let you do whatever you want because she'll feel guilty about uprooting her baby, particularly if you're moving in with her fiancé who keeps a potbellied pig.

No matter the box or the occasion, always remember the most important rule of box-steading. Be adorable. One thing is for certain: Any cat looking cute in a cardboard box keeps her box for that much longer, and has lots more boxes in her future.

THINGS THAT ARE NOT BOXES THAT YOU SHOULD BE IN

Grocery Bag: What's in that bag? Are you in that bag? If not, get in there!

Cooler: Your comfort is more important than the temperature of the beer.

Colander: These are cozy and perfectly cat-sized, and besides, spaghetti isn't even delicious.

Laundry Basket: Nothing improves a pair of dress slacks like your fur.

Bathroom Sink: Your person can brush her teeth just as well in that one in the kitchen.

Overturned Cowboy Hat: No matter how angry it's making that good ol' boy, you're golden as long as the girls swoon over you.

Extraordinary Cats in History—Part I

A ll cats love to leave their mark on things. People, furniture, books, even whole houses can be declared cat property and, once that happens, never be taken away.

Marking a place in history is another matter. To be remembered forever takes more than a simple brush against destiny, and it's definitely not as easy as snagging a video-game system by rubbing your face on the controller.

What follows are tales of those who earned their place in the annals of history with persistence, courage, intelligence, and cunning. These cats will always be revered. They are extraordinary.

FRED—UNDERCOVER DETECTIVE CAT

While law enforcement agencies have employed many dogs, the number of cat cops has been much smaller. This is mainly due to the fact that cats aren't particularly keen on intractable rules and generally prefer more flexible guidelines. There is, however, one absolute law that must be obeyed: Anyone practicing veterinary medicine had better be board certified and licensed by the state. A cat named Fred discovered that law being broken and decided to do something about it.

When Fred was a kitten living on the mean streets of New York City, he had a host of health problems, and it didn't appear there was much hope for him. Luckily, Fred was rescued by Animal Care & Control. He was nursed back to health and eventually became part of a loving family.

Fred's adopted family worked in the New York district attorney's office. One case under investigation concerned a phony veterinarian operating without proper training or licensing. The DA's office was contacted by the owner of a dog named Burt who had endured an unsafe and unnecessary surgery.

A brief investigation revealed that Burt was not the first animal to be victimized by this quack. Less than a year after being plucked from the streets, Fred was enlisted to help bring down the perpetrator. He signed on without reservation. The guy had to be stopped.

A sting was set in motion. First, police outfitted a mock apartment in Brooklyn with concealed microphones and cameras. Then a detective contacted the phony vet and inquired about having her cat neutered. When the appointment was scheduled, the district attorney's office sent in Fred as their undercover cat.

Fred, Undercover Cat for the New York district attorney's office

The subject arrived at the apartment and agreed to neuter Fred for the sum of $135. The trap was sprung. As he tried to leave with Fred in a cat carrier, waiting detectives cuffed him.

Following the arrest, Fred received many honors. He appeared at press conferences wearing his DA badge, received a Law Enforcement Appreciation Award, and was even presented the Mayor's Alliance Award by Mary Tyler Moore and Bernadette Peters on Broadway.

It is with a heavy heart that we tell you Fred passed away in 2006. His death remains a tragic loss, but it is comforting to know Fred will never be forgotten.

Extraordinary Cats in History—Part I

ALICE—THE CAT WHO PLAYS GUITAR BETTER THAN JIMI HENDRIX

As anyone who has ever poked around on YouTube will attest, cats can play the piano. The world is sadly unaware, however, of a freaky cat named Alice. Not only is she the first feline to play the guitar, but Alice can also jam better than Jimi Hendrix.

Alice lives in Sandusky, Ohio—a long ways from Jimi Hendrix's hometown of Seattle, Washington, but the two do share a birthday, November 27th. Alice knows this because her person, Danny B., makes it a point to tell her at almost any opportunity.

Danny B. has been an aspiring guitarist for fourteen years, and sometime in 2003 he inspired Alice to take up the instrument.

One night she watched as Danny B. practiced, her ears twitching each time he hit a bad note. He got progressively more discouraged, eventually throwing the guitar down in frustration.

After running out to the garage for a little while, he came back and popped in his *Woodstock* DVD for the 167th time. As Danny B. muttered about how great Hendrix was, Alice sniffed around his guitar and pawed at the strings. She liked how it felt but got scared at the noise and ran to Danny B.'s lap, curling up with him on the couch to watch how Hendrix did it.

For five years Alice followed that same basic schedule. Every night after Danny B. was done practicing, she lounged with him on the couch and studied Hendrix intently until the pizza came.

In time, Alice began to understand where Jimi was coming from. She got the guitar and started making noises that weren't frightening. Cats started to come from all over to peer in the window and watch her jam. With her eyes closed and head tilted back, Alice put on the show she learned from Hendrix, but then took it a step further.

Instead of just playing with her teeth and behind her back, Alice perfected the trick of using her tail, something that not even Jimi dreamt of doing. Having five claws on each paw meant she could play without a pick. With this technique Alice brought a whole new meaning to the term "guitar shredding."

Danny B. still doesn't know Alice can play, because she waits until he's gone to work at the coin-operated Laundromat before cranking up the amplifier. Lately she has been putting the finishing touches on her album, *Salmon: Bold As Love*. It's a shame the human world will be deprived of it, but her cat fans in Sandusky are preparing to be blown away. Rumor has it that her use of a meow-meow pedal is unbelievable.

Cats and Arch-Villains

—————— 🐾 ——————

The film industry has long acknowledged the relationship between cats and arch-villains. Whether it is the white Persian held by James Bond's nemesis, Ernst Stavro Blofeld, or the cat behind the desk of Don Corleone, or Lucifer, the companion of Cinderella's evil stepmother, the presence of a feline is often a tipping point between regular villain and arch-villain. Though these examples are fictional, like all great movie conventions, they are rooted in reality. Rumor has it that Benedict Arnold was convinced to turn traitor thanks to a stray with a taste for British pudding, and according to intelligence reports leaked from North Korea, dictator Kim Jong Il receives counsel from an all-Siamese advisory panel. The dynamic between cat and arch-villain is a complex one, and perhaps the most symbiotic of all interspecies relationships.

World domination is not a single-person enterprise. Villains who aspire to more than the occasional petty small-town bank heist know they need allies. As an animal that naturally maintains dominance over all it surveys, cats are uniquely qualified to advise these evil power-seekers on topics such as double-crossing, silencing do-gooders, and constructing a W80 thermonuclear warhead that can be deployed via cruise missile using the BGM-109G Gryphon GLCM.

The decision to ally oneself with an arch-villain, however, is a difficult one. First of all, helping a human take control of a world that is al-

---

A DAY IN THE LIFE OF AN ARCH-VILLAIN'S CAT

6:00 A.M. **Wake up evil army by stepping on all of their faces**
8:45 A.M. **Stare at shark tank for twenty minutes before selecting which one you want for breakfast**

---

ready ours seems a bit silly, but sometimes a power-sharing agreement is preferable to protracted conflict. There are several important questions to consider before aiding any diabolical plot:

- What kind of food is the dastardly genius offering in exchange for your services? Are we talking plain-old canned chicken hearts and liver, or is there a promise of fresh grouper? Chances are good your involvement will result in the subjugation of all mankind, so demand that food be at least four out of five stars.
- How competent is the arch-villain? Azrael was a strong, proud cat, but his alliance with the bumbling evil wizard Gargamel perpetually made him look foolish. Being undone and embarrassed by a piddling group of blue half-men like the Smurfs is something no cat should ever endure. Before you sign on with an evildoer, request to see a résumé of past malevolent deeds. Additionally, have him detail his five- and ten-year plans. Find out if he hopes to rule over a hemisphere or if his ambition begins and ends with blowing up a dam. Remember, arch-villains need you more than you need them. Be selective.
- Does the arch-villain have plans for domination beyond Earth? This is a critical question. If the rogue is setting up Moon bases, building menacing spaceships, or developing intergalactic teleportation technology, cats may finally be able to search for the succulent alien fish thought to exist in the frozen Venusian ocean.

A DAY IN THE LIFE OF AN ARCH-VILLAIN'S CAT

9:30 A.M. Get on the horn with the South American outpost and see how the construction of the satellite field in the heart of the Amazon is coming along

Noon Chase slowly rolling smoke bomb around

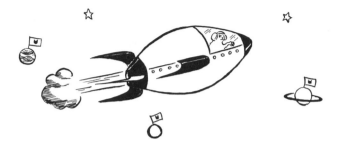

- How comfortable is the arch-villain's lap? As his official cat, you will be spending nearly all of your time there. He'll need to keep in contact with you twenty-four hours a day, seven days a week. There is no time off in the world-domination business. The last thing you want is to be stuck on a bony pelvis. Make sure to inspect the thighs of the arch-villain before signing on. If there's a little heft on the lower half, you'll be in good shape, but make sure it's not too rotund. You don't want to be the nearest thing in reach of a Jabba the Hutt–type when he starts feeling hungry.

If you ultimately decide to align with an arch-villain, there are certain protocols to follow. You won't always see eye-to-eye, but direct confrontation is messy and time-consuming. Also, it's best not to rile homicidal maniacs. If you want to get your way or make a suggestion, there is an easy, peaceful method to communicate ideas:

A DAY IN THE LIFE OF AN ARCH-VILLAIN'S CAT

12:15 P.M. Hiss at Interpol agent who threw smoke bomb as he engages in hand-to-hand combat with henchmen
3:00 P.M. Play with rope that is keeping Interpol agent tied to a chair

---

1. When you are in the lap of the arch-villain, he will have a natural compulsion to pet you.
2. As the arch-villain strokes your fur, begin to meditate on the given situation. Let's say, for example, that he leads an organized-crime syndicate and some sad sack is in the office, begging for forgiveness after once again failing to pay his weekly tribute. If the groveling human happens to run a decent bakery or sells high-quality meats, he will likely offer food in lieu of cash. Visualize the arch-villain's henchmen refraining from taking a baseball bat to the guy's legs.

A DAY IN THE LIFE OF AN ARCH-VILLAIN'S CAT

6:30 P.M. **Climb to top of watchtower, consider signaling to clueless guards that SEAL Team 3 is approaching; nap instead**
8:00 P.M. **Go back down to command center to see who's in charge now**

---

3. Once you've made the decision to show mercy, a special glycoprotein with encoded instructions is released through your fur. The unique skin of arch-villains can absorb feline glycoprotein, so when their fingertips make contact with you,

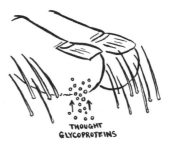

THOUGHT
GLYCOPROTEINS

the instructions travel through their bloodstream and into their brains. Once there, your message is received and your bidding is carried out.
4. In this case, the order to show mercy is communicated, and soon you will be snacking on cannoli and sopressata.

Perhaps you are asking: Why not ally with a superhero instead of an arch-villain? It really comes down to shared goals. Very rarely does one hear of a superhero who aims to control all space and time. They just don't have the same drive and ambition as their wicked adversaries. There is, however, one caveat to consider. All arch-villains have an expiration date. Eventually the hubris from which they derive power causes their downfall. If you find yourself in a flaming underground bunker as your arch-villain and a super-spy are battling it out, don't be afraid to switch sides. You are under no obligation to go down with the secret island base. Jump on the arch-villain's back and start clawing like crazy while the good guy blasts him with a laser gun. Then prepare to be whisked away to safety and honored for your heroics. This new standing will put you in a good position to become a democratically elected universal ruler—so either way, it's win-win.

Groom, Groom, Groom, Groom, Groom, Groom, Groom

Today's cat is busier than ever. A crush of distractions and ever-increasing responsibilities compete for our limited attention. Scan the ceiling for bugs. Check the sink for dirty dishes. Tear apart that new bouquet of flowers on the coffee table. Just thinking about it all is enough to make you crazy.

Being beautifully groomed may seem like yet another chore, but a cat's appearance can't be put at the bottom of the list.

Life should never get in the way of your beauty. Just groom, groom, groom, groom, groom, groom, groom right through a busy day.

MIDSECTION

Properly wedging in between your sleeping person's knees sometimes takes quite a few tries. Don't let an opportunity for a good midsection cleaning go by as she tosses back and forth. She's soundly half-asleep, so go ahead and slurp all you want.

PAWS

You've been scratching at the underside of the mattress for fifteen minutes straight. Take a break now and then to rid your lovely mitts of all that dust while your person pleads for you to come out of there.

BEHIND THE EARS

When smacking the bedroom door to gain entry, stop occasionally to hear if your person is climbing out of bed. That's a good time to clean well behind the ears before resuming scratching at the door until it opens.

UNDER THE CHIN

The shower curtain requires cleaning again and your person is too busy blow-drying her hair to be bothered. Licking it spotless falls to you and that's a big job. Use the water that collects in the fur under your chin as a moisturizer. You'll look so good leaving the bathroom no one will ever guess how much work you did.

SHOULDERS

Don't be tempted to stand idly watching your person try to find her keys before she leaves the house. It's an entertaining way to spend ten minutes, but not really the best use of your time. Here's a time-saving tip: The moment she starts to wave goodbye, take a serious interest in your shoulders. After all, the show's pretty much over and there's no point in just standing there.

FACE

As you're getting comfortable for the ride to Planet Naptune, squeeze in a quick scrub of your pretty face. You'll be a more attractive snoozer and also discover that the dream flying saucer goes even faster with slick whiskers.

BOTTOM

When your person returns home you're expected to sit down and listen to her day. It's just as easy to feign paying attention while cleaning your bottom.

Groom, Groom, Groom, Groom, Groom, Groom, Groom

The Laws of Petting

In our nation's colonial days, cats were safely ensconced inside homes, but they were having trouble getting any real attention. Humans were so busy running around crabbing about tea, electrocuting kites, and ladling out liberty that they had little space in their schedules for cuddle sessions. On the off chance a human happened to be lying around the house, it was because he was too woozy from copious medicinal leechings to be out making history, let alone paying attention to cat antics.

However, it just so happened that these blood-deprived humans also had a habit of passing out and knocking over kerosene lamps. While cats were annoyed at having to constantly lick them awake and guide them to safety through walls of flame, it was because of these heroics that humans finally stopped taking cats for granted.

Even with this victory, the situation failed to substantially improve. Cats were getting attention, but it stunk. They bristled at the occasional ham-fisted pat the man of the house dished out, or wriggled frantically against strangleholds the children inflicted.

Cats everywhere grew increasingly dissatisfied with the frequency and quality of attention received, and soon fervent but anonymously penned pamphlets began to circulate. The most heralded tract was "A Petition for Proper Petting."

The Laws of Petting

Kitty Cat of Virginia

A groundswell of popular support for these notions gained steam. Our Founding Felines knew that to make cohabitation work, they must firmly establish the fundamentals governing affection, and thus a group of respected elders was convened. Known as the Angora Assembly, this distinguished delegation included some of our most famous historical figures, such as one-eyed tuxedo cat Puss of Massachusetts, fey long-hair Kitty Cat of New York, dander-plagued Cat of Delaware, ginger states-cat Puss Puss of New Jersey, and Atticus Broome of Pennsylvania.

After much debate on human hand technique, an initial draft of the Laws of Petting was drawn up.

However, dissenting member Kitty Cat of Virginia (no relation to Kitty Cat of New York), a foul-tempered Siamese, argued that this historic document must not merely illustrate the manner in which we shall be petted but should likewise establish a cat's basic rights to be petted when, where, and for however long she wants.

After a great deal of hissing and quick smacks to one another's heads, these leaders finally came to agreement, and so ratified the Laws of Petting.

To this day these Laws protect and govern our right to be petted in such manner and at such times as we require and demand.

PREAMBLE TO THE LAWS OF PETTING

We pussycats hereby decree that in order to maintain tranquility and harmony in the relations betwixt cat and human, it is resolved and ordained that cats shall be accorded these basic rights when being stroked, scratched, or snuggled.

Article I: When ye shall walk within reaching distance of a human, said human is commanded to pet even if she clutch a grocery sack or race to extinguish a gristle flare on the stove. Should ye be occupying a stair in the middle of the staircase, ye must at minimum be accorded a quick skritch before being stepped over. Upon a headbutt or figure eight through a human's legs, ye shall be petted in many varieties until ye be satisfied or become distracted by a thimble or an object of similar interest.

Article II: Scratches behind the ears and neck shall at all times be dictated by random turns of thy head, and the human's hand shall migrate accordingly.

Article III: If thy belly be exposed, thy belly must be rubbed, except should ye be violently averse to having thy belly rubbed and take a swipe at the human, then thy belly should most definitely be left alone.

Article IV: Aye, shall ye be scratched right in that sweet spot by the tail!

Article V: Shall ye rest upon a lap, ye must be provided with a bounty of strokes and scratches, which shall include, without limitation, thy ears and face, back and tail, and for a time that ye shall determine. Nay, no potboiler, nor loom, nor cross-stitch sampler shall come in the way of a cat's rights in these regards.

Article VI: Ye shall indicate petting is complete by wandering hither or jumping forth from a lap. However, shall ye take a bite of the hand, a swipe at the arm, or a full-on mad-eyed lunge at the human's face, this, too, shall indicate that all further petting activities must cease. Ye shall not be punished, and the human should very well know what she did wrong.

The ratification of the assembly of these cats, whose exact number is not determined as they oft wandered in and out of the Hall, shall be sufficient for the establishment of these Laws between humans and cats so ratifying the same.

Though no humans were invited to the Assembly, these Laws they are duly bound to uphold.

Later these Laws were amended, and the subjects of these amendments highlight the impassioned debates that came with great changes in our society throughout history.

1st Amendment: Belly rubs may not be used as a sneaky ploy to clip tummy dreadlocks.

2nd Amendment: Cat brushes may hereby be used in place of hands so long as we be allowed to chase and consume the chunks of fur that may float into the air.

3rd Amendment: Grooming mitts are terrifying and are hereby prohibited.

4th Amendment: All female humans shall hereby have those amazing new scratchy things called acrylic nails applied and they shall pretend these nails are race cars on our backs.

5th Amendment: After having finally tried one, we hereby repeal the 3rd Amendment.

6th Amendment: The rights accorded in Article V are hereby declared extended so that these, too, shall not infringe on a cat's rights described therein: *People* magazine, microwave timer, reality-program finale, phone call from ex-boyfriend, or online game of Scrabble.

Secrets of Daredevil Cats

ⓐ

Cats aren't shy about risking life and limb in pursuit of thrills. One day it's a blink-of-an-eye stunt, taking you from the couch to the coffee table, off a chair, and onto a wheeled footrest that skids across the room. The next, it's a headline-grabbing leap out the window of a high-rise building. Either way, you are awarded the awestruck admiration accorded all audacious cats.

But have you ever asked yourself how we physically and mentally pull off such amazing feats? What is it that makes us capable of walking out on the ledge, walking off said ledge, and living to revel in glory?

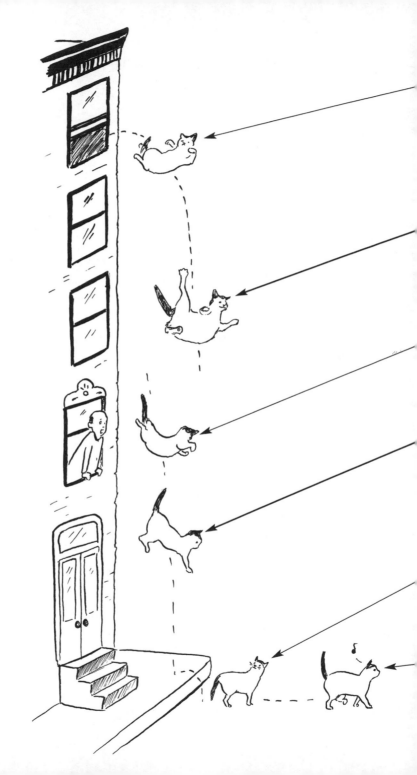

FEAR OF HEIGHTS? HA!
No cat afraid of extreme heights is much of a daredevil. Humans have named our ability to stay poised at such elevations "High-Rise Syndrome." We just call it "Walking Around." Thinking we might hurt ourselves, humans try to protect us against our "overconfidence" with respect to lofty perches. It's always hilarious to be called "overconfident" by a human.

NO COLLARBONE? NO PROBLEM
Cats do have clavicles but they are nonfunctional, a chief reason we're able to perform the neat trick of squeezing through impossibly tight spaces. It also isn't a bad thing when you're landing from a fall. Evel Knievel had two collarbones and broke them both.

RIGHT EVERY TIME (PART ONE)
Why does a cat always land on its feet? One answer is rooted in physics, which requires understanding concepts of rotational motion. It's much easier just to talk about the Righting Reflex, which is fun to say over and over.

RIGHT EVERY TIME (PART TWO)
The Righting Reflex is what allows us to orient our bodies to keep from tumbling through the air while falling. It is performed by bending at the middle so that the front half of the body rotates on an axis opposite to the rear half. The front legs come around first, then the rear. Everything is as it should be as we streak toward the ground for a perfect landing.

CATS HAVE A NONFATAL TERMINAL VELOCITY
A falling cat cannot exceed 60 mph. This is an important reason we're able to survive long falls. Small size, light bone structure, and a coat of fur all help keep our terminal velocity low. By comparison, a human's terminal velocity is 130 mph. When it comes to walking away from a multistory landing, bigger is definitely not better.

INABILITY TO FEEL REGRET
Regret is not a feeling cats have to deal with, and that little fact frees us up to do some just plain crazy stuff. Without having to regret a decision, we're always able to go for it!

Secrets of Daredevil Cats

Wake Up!

————————— 🐾 —————————

You're winding down from a long night of diving across the hall after a coat button. Now the sun is coming up and you could use a little snack. But that bacon-grease-filled pan you were counting on is gone from the stove. And no matter how hard you look, there aren't any food nuggets hiding under your dish. Actually, the more you think about it, you aren't just peckish, you are STARVING! Literally wasting away before no one's eyes! Where is your person? How can she be contentedly bundled under a bunch of blankets, drooling and snoring? Doesn't she know you could die of hunger any second?

If you could feed yourself, you would, but frankly it is impossible. Your person purchased a can opener designed in a discriminatory manner so as not to accommodate paws. Those newfangled pouches she brought home are like titanium to teeth. And that refrigerator she hides food in is an impenetrable Fort Knox of delicious leftover chicken fajita and cream cheese.

Of course there's dry food in the bowl, but you're keeping that for later.

That leaves only one possible option. To save your very life your person needs to get up immediately and open *something*! Well, something you're actually in the mood for, perhaps involving giblets, or a seafood component. Except, you're not really feeling whitefish this morning, unless maybe if the whitefish is part of a deep-sea medley. But that's a bridge you'll cross when you come to it. Right now, you just need to focus on the problem at hand.

While shrieking up a storm might seem to be the most straightforward attention-getter, you know that usually results in you being tossed out into the ol' hallway with the door slammed in your face. Instead, try some of these more subtle ways to wake her up and get you fed (in escalating order):

Face Touching: Ever so gently—no claws—place a paw on her cheek. Now smoosh, then release. Smoosh, then release. We recommend ten reps of three.

Lick a Plastic Bag: Lick, lick. Wasn't that annoying to read? Imagine what it sounds like if you just rolled in a few hours ago from margarita night out with the girls.

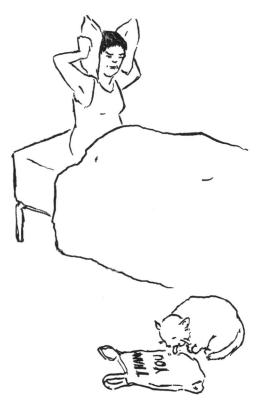

Plastic department-store bags strewn around the bedroom floor aren't just fun, they can be staunch allies in your quest to get grub. In the event your person is careful to hide her purchases and dispose of the bag evidence, a lamp shade or dry-cleaning bag are acceptable substitutes.

Whack Something Repeatedly: Using your paw, rapidly whack at something in the room. It's important that the something you choose to whack, in turn smacks into something else and makes a noise—a really irritating noise that you can commit to maintaining for at least ten minutes. The blinds or a hinged closet door are popular options. If nothing in the room happens to fit the bill, scratching the wallpaper works just as well.

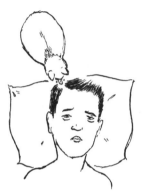

Hair Chewing and Licking: Start by nibbling the ends, build up to a gnaw and finish with a series of aggressive tugs. Should your person have short hair unsuitable for chewing, treat her to a full head grooming instead. These techniques are designed to really get her attention, but they may well get you kicked off the bed. If she doesn't get up and follow, jump back up there and move on to the next, and final, step.

Hand Licking/Biting: Your sandpapery tongue will awaken her briefly, and she'll probably be touched by your little display of affection. That's the time to drive home the immediacy of your desperate situation with a startling nip. Be careful not to bite too hard and draw blood. You need that hand operational for food-dispensing duties. If for some reason one bite isn't enough, be prepared for an encore or two.

At this point she'll probably realize her alarm is going to go off in thirty minutes anyway, so she might as well just get out of bed and feed you.

But what if she actually does dole out plain old whitefish? Just walk away and take a nap on that big warm spot on the bed.

Stowaway Stories

Cats are born with wanderlust. We all crave the romance of the highway, spirited sailing adventures, and the chance to shed all over the most opulent salons of Paris. Even the most mild among us generally enjoy rubbing on new people, staring at different cultures, and refusing to eat local cuisines. But some cats don't just dream of doing these things—they get out there and do them, by stowing away.

Stowing away is the perfect choice for a cat who's ready to see the world beyond her person's home, without the exhausting preparation and expense that normally comes with traveling. It's easy enough for any cat to do. Just fall asleep in something, wait for it to start moving, and you're on your way! No reservations or ticket required.*

*Note: If you wake up and have failed to move, you may have fallen asleep in a bed. Get up and try again.

These are the real-life tales of three brave stowaways, and what happened to them out on the open road.

ZIGGY

Ziggy was a fluffy white cat with two different-colored eyes, just like his namesake, Ziggy Stardust. But Ziggy wasn't a rock star from outer space. He was a kitty from Haifa, Israel, with a thirst for culinary adventure. So one day, he curled up in a shipping crate, and let Fate take him where it would. Ziggy didn't much care where he landed, so long as the living was easy and the cuisine memorable. He ended up on a seventeen-day, 2,000-mile voyage across the sea to the town of Lancashire, England. Lancashire's known for lots of things. Cat food is not one of them. Ziggy refused to let the dubious destination dampen his enthusiasm. When his crate opened, he darted out and headed straight to the local pub, where he enjoyed a surprisingly good pint of Lancashire ale and the tastiest black pudding he ever had. It may have taken seventeen days to get there, but Ziggy thought every bite was worth it.

GRACIE MAE

Looking for a nice spot to snooze, Florida tabby Gracie Mae stumbled upon a cushy box filled with clothes. Wasn't she in luck! As Gracie climbed in, she briefly wondered why she hadn't noticed this choice spot before. Gracie soon fell sound asleep. That's when the strange dreams started. A cozy box . . . a car ride . . . an airport . . . a noisy machine that took her picture.

It was only when Gracie awoke in a cramped, dark space that she realized it wasn't a dream at all. She *had* been in the airport. That cozy box she'd climbed into was her person's suitcase, and he hadn't noticed her when he finished packing. Instead, he'd zipped it up and checked the bag with the airline. Now Gracie was in the cargo section of an airplane—and she was the only one who knew it!

After a chilly trip without snacks or beverages, Gracie's plane finally landed in Fort Worth, Texas. She took a few rough rides around the luggage carousel before the bag was picked up. Finally, she thought, this whole mess will be sorted out.

But the mess was far from over. The suitcase was picked up—but not by Gracie's person. A stranger mistook the bag for hers, took it home, and opened it up. Gracie and the stranger were equally surprised. The stranger was not expecting to find a cat, and Gracie had never seen someone wearing a ten-gallon hat.

The lady checked the tag and called Gracie's person, who was equally shocked to hear that his cat was in the Longhorn state. Gracie was sent back on her way, but not before a little bit of sightseeing and a hearty taste of Texas-style chili.

MIRACLE

A little gray stray from Newark, New Jersey, Miracle had always wanted to go to Philadelphia. He wanted to run up and down the steps outside the art museum like his idol, Rocky Balboa.

There was only one problem. Miracle didn't know where Philadelphia was. So when he heard about an SUV that was taking something called the "turnpike" in that direction, he climbed underneath to hitch a ride.

Little Miracle made it some seventy miles before another driver noticed him clinging to the car and frantically waved down the driver of the SUV. Everyone was amazed that Miracle had avoided serious injury—one bad bump could have easily killed him. When the good people got him out he was missing a claw, and his paws were a little singed—but other than those little things, he was A-OK. That's why they named him Miracle.

After that, an animal services agency put Miracle up for adoption. Within days the tough little kitty had a loving home. Miracle still hasn't made it to Philly, but we know he will someday. He's already proved to be one heck of a fighter.

Relatives and Ancestors

You might be surprised to learn that the domestic cat (you) is not the only kind of cat in existence. On the contrary, there are dozens of other cat species in this great world of ours, and you are related to all of them. Like relatives everywhere, they have quirks and foibles you need to be aware of, lest any decide to drop by unexpectedly. It hasn't happened to anybody we know yet, but it's better to be prepared. With that in mind, here is a clear, unbiased look at what we've heard about the other cats of the world.

LEOPARDS

Perhaps you've heard the expression "A leopard can't change its spots." It's a stupid saying, because why would any cat want to change anything about itself? It does, however, give you the most pertinent information about leopards: They have spots, and are stubborn. Once they've made up their minds, they never change them. If a leopard wants to go out to grab a gazelle while he's visiting you, don't try telling him that there are no gazelles in your part of the world. It would be a waste of breath. Let him go. Maybe he'll catch a deer or a cow and think it's a gazelle, and then you'll both be happy. This brings us to our next point, which is that leopards are good hunters. They live in Africa.

CHEETAHS

Cheetahs apparently also have spots, but for some reason we've never heard anyone make up clever adages about them. What we do know, thanks to passing by the television during a program, is that cheetahs are very fast. Like, if Superman's cat and a cheetah were to get in a race, the cheetah would win. This speed helps them win Olympic gold medals in track, and makes them handy for parcel delivery. They are also annoying show-offs who want to race all the time. If you humor them by participating, they will win and want to race again. And again. They just get superexcited about running. The best thing you can do is send them off to see how long it takes them to run around the block a hundred times.

TIGERS

Tigers like to swim. SWIM! That means they like to go IN the water and stay there for an extended period of time. Cuckoo! You'd think, based on that, there wouldn't be any relation, but one look at them pretty much confirms it. They may be huge (bigger than all your other relatives, even),

but the family resemblance is there. The sharp incisors. The whiskers. The ears. The twitchy tail. But they have stripes like a zebra. Zebras like swimming. Zebras are also bigger than most cats. Therefore, it is obvious that a tiger is half cat and half zebra. They're still your relatives, though, so be respectful, which is actually easy because tigers are very polite. They won't leave big muddy paw prints in your house, and they will usually bring a carcass they picked up on the way over.

JAGUARS

Jaguars are laid-back, and, with their keen sense of hearing, they make good listeners. They are also excellent at preparing meals, making them great guests. Don't believe us? If one should stop by the house and you don't have anything to eat, he will apologize for dropping by unexpectedly and whip up a delicious five-course meal just from stuff you had lying around. Also—this is really cool—they have the strongest jaws of all cats and can bite right through a skull. Yeah, gross, but cool. They also have some pretty funny stories about living in the jungle. Like the one about the monkey that rode the giraffe like a cowboy. We'd tell you the whole thing, but it's better when they do it.

BLAH BLAH BLAH
BLAH BLAH
BLAH BLAH
BLAH

LIONS

Lions will be the first to tell you that they are Kings of the Jungle. Don't tell them otherwise or you'll have a roaring fit on your hands. Definitely don't point out that they don't live in the jungle, either. They hate that. The main thing about lions is that they are really full of themselves. Get a little meat in them and they go on and on about how important they are and how much work it is to keep order in their kingdom, and how they are so important. They don't ask how your day was at all. Man lions have a ring of long hair around their necks called a mane. They hang out in groups called prides. They live in Africa, as well.

OCELOTS

Size-wise, ocelots are somewhere between us and a jaguar. Because of their in-between status, they just want to fit in, so they'll do anything for a laugh. That's great, for a while, but it can get pretty annoying when it's nothing but *The Ocelot Show*. You usually have to do what they want to do, otherwise they won't show up. Besides those traits, they're not that bad.

BOBCATS

Of all your relatives, the bobcat is the most likely to pay you a visit, partially since they are the most closely related, but mainly because they live on the same landmass as you. Don't expect a lot from them. Visits can be awkward and stilted, since they are loners by nature. Usually, they'll sit quietly and smoke. If you try to engage one in conversation, he'll just answer "Yes" or "No" or "Rabbits." The jury is still out on whether this is because they are stuck up or just shy. Just remember to keep your chin up and be nice. Maybe you can get them to open up with kindness.

SABER-TOOTHED TIGERS

Saber-toothed tigers were our way-way-way-back ancestors. Like, before your mom and her mom and her mom. That old. As such, it's hard to say what they were really like. Based on cave drawings and pictures in museum books, they lived with cavemen and had huge teeth. They probably fought dinosaurs, and when they purred, it could have sounded like a motorcycle. Since they're extinct, there's not much of a chance that one will stop by. If one does, make sure to take a picture, because no one will believe you otherwise.

Choosing the Perfect Gift

There's a persistent myth that cats are selfish creatures. Nothing could be further from the truth. Felines love to show their appreciation for friendly gestures. We adore giving gifts nearly as much as we enjoy getting them, and it's one of the many things we excel at.

Though some cats find public displays of affection distasteful, gift giving is universally thought of as a classy way to show you care. If you just want to say thanks for a good scratch under the chin, a little taste of half-and-half, or a timely can of food, it can usually be accomplished with an affectionate head butt. For the times when you need to say more, give a gift. Here are some wonderful gifts to help you mark almost any occasion.

BIRDS

A perennial gift and timeless cat classic. With their soft feathers and bright plumage, birds never go out of style and won't fail to elicit a spirited response. Leave one at your person's feet for a gift she'll never forget. As always, presentation is important. Scatter feathers leading up to the side of the bed, to the edge of a relaxing bubble bath, or just let her find it on her own! Whether she's celebrating an engagement or anniversary, getting over a bad breakup, or simply wearing sweats and bawling in between spoonfuls of mocha-chip ice cream, the versatile bird is just the thing to lift her spirits.

MICE

Sometimes you want a gift that does the talking for you. When you just don't have the meows for what it is you're trying to say, say it with a mouse. You can give your person a mouse for any reason, but the best reason to give one is for no reason at all. A mouse is the perfect way for the quiet cat to say, "I love you, just because." Giving a mouse isn't a showy gesture. It's a reminder that you care enough to keep your person's home rodent free. Place one of these guys in your water dish, or, better yet, tucked neatly into a running shoe, as a special surprise.

INSECTS

From the mighty cicada to the lowly cockroach, these small tokens of affection are unrivaled in variety and appearance. They come in a broad range of colors, so be sure to choose one that suits your person's tastes and matches their décor. Bugs are also crunchy and delicious, and you will most certainly want to eat them, but hold back if you can. Instead, chew them up just enough to show you've put some effort in to it. Give insects whenever someone gets a new job, or if there's a new addition to the family, but especially if your person is moving to a new home. Insects make great housewarming gifts.

A word of caution: It may seem odd, but some people react poorly when presented with a bird, mouse, or insect. Even more bizarre is how they tend to do this most when you've actually gone through the extra trouble of snapping the neck just so, getting the carcass good and bloody, and artfully spreading the guts around.

Does a poor response mean it's a bad gift? Absolutely not. Cats have impeccable taste. We never give bad gifts. Your human might not like it at first, but eventually she'll come around.

Should you be unable to obtain a wildlife gift due to limited availability, here are a few more options.

RIBBON

It's often said you should give the gift you hope to get, and who wouldn't want a satiny, twirly piece of brightly colored ribbon? The color is up to you, but you'll generally want to keep the ribbon about six to eight inches in length. Anything less will seem stingy, but too much and you're bound to seem ostentatious. And if money's a little tight? You can make your own ribbon by shredding wide strips off curtains, drapes, ties, blouses, bedsheets, and fancy dresses, or just about any item your human already loves.

There's an added bonus to giving this gift: Most humans don't really know what to do with a piece of ribbon, except give it back to you to play with. So this one pays for itself.

GIFT CARD

It's rare, but there are some cats out there who just aren't very good at gift giving. Getting your human a gift card to her favorite store probably isn't the best you can do, but at least it's something.

BALLPOINT PEN CAP

The ballpoint pen cap is a popular choice for graduations, or when your person receives a promotion. They're usually not hard to find, but people are always looking for them and are usually pleased to receive one. Of course, other

things you find in the home, such as pencils, bottle tops, paper clips, and the like might suit your person better. Don't be afraid to experiment.

YOU

That's right—you! No matter what the occasion, you're the perfect gift. You don't cost much, you're always the right size, and you know your person already likes you. Just walk on over to her and offer up your belly for a real good rub. Then purr like the dickens. The only thing about this gift? It's non-returnable. But don't worry about that. You're not going anywhere.

Famous Cats of the Funny Pages

When it comes to entertainment, cats get short shrift. There isn't a lot out there that accurately depicts the breadth and richness of our lives. Sure, entertainment producers are always eager to cash in on our popularity by shoehorning the word "cat" in the title, but it's usually nothing more than false advertising.

Take, for example, songs about cats. It turns out that "Cat's in the Cradle" isn't even about cats, but rather the strained relationship between a human son and his self-obsessed dad, who probably doesn't even own a cat. If you're looking for a good movie about cats, the cultured feline might choose *Cat on a Hot Tin Roof,* only to find out that it's mainly Burl Ives shouting. The musical *Cats* is nothing more than a gaudy burlesque, a minstrel show of people in catface makeup. Television shows? Forget about it.

Where are we to turn for a positive cat role model?

To the stuff that lines our litter box, that's where. The comics page has long been a haven for cats looking for a voice of sanity in the media. Not all strips are accurate, but they're a lot more entertaining than the ones about politically minded talking ducks. They almost always make you laugh, but sometimes, they make you think. Unfortunately, cats in the comics are often paired with dogs, pointing to a dynamic that barely exists in real life. A comic artist who wanted to get rich would do very well to create a strip that focused on a cat sleeping or tossing a toy around. That would be the funniest comic ever.

These are some of the most influential cats who have appeared in the medium.

KRAZY KAT

Krazy Kat, drawn by George Herriman, is lauded as one of the all-time great comic strips by human nerds. Marked by its surreal southwestern setting, its playful placement of panels and poetic language, the strip stands as a high-water mark for these comics aficionados. In reality, its laughable characterization of cats still rubs a lot of felines the wrong way. Krazy Kat, the lead character, is in love with a German mouse named Ignatz. Most cats do love mice, but for dinner, not romantically. This lovesickness is probably what makes her krazy. Ignatz hates Krazy, and often throws a brick at her, as if a tiny mouse could raise a brick, let alone hurl it with any force or accuracy. Even if a mouse were able to achieve such a feat, that mouse would be batted around like a superball shortly thereafter. Although not true to a cat's spirit, we do owe a great deal to the fact that Krazy Kat opened the door for other cats to follow.

HEATHCLIFF

The 1973 appearance of *Heathcliff* really set the standard for a sympathetic depiction of cats in the comics. Though his actions were often less than accurate— such as how he brazenly flips the lids off garbage cans instead of stealthily pushing them off and hiding until the noise dies down—Heathcliff captures the essence of being a cat, albeit a brazen tom, and not a refined house cat. Unlike the comic cats that have followed, he does it without uttering a word in the human tongue. As of late, Heathcliff has been given to performing more human activities than in the strip's heyday. This may diminish the character, but not the standard he's set.

GARFIELD

Without a doubt, Garfield is the ten-ton gorilla in the comics room. Or ten-ton cat! Garfield is fat, lazy, and proud of it; he hates Mondays and loves lasagna. He spends a lot of time sitting around the house, and that kitten Nermal really gets on his nerves! Garfield's penchant for eating is definitely on the mark, although he often eats foods that most cats would steer clear of. His relation with Odie the dog approaches the sublime; Garfield is definitely the boss, but will periodically cave in to a display of affection. One major flaw is that it's never really explained how his dim-witted person, Jon, can understand him when Garfield is thinking, not talking. In this respect, it's more fantasy than an accurate depiction of a cat's life, though if more owners had the telepathic link that Garfield and Jon apparently share, the world would be a much better place.

BILL THE CAT

Has anyone ever said so much with such a limited vocabulary? With a simple "ack" and "pbbbtttht," *Bloom County*'s Bill the Cat charmed his way into American hearts. Hairballs, litter boxes, a deep-rooted love of inactivity—Bill puts it all out there for cats and people alike to see, and damn the consequences. He's a legend, a celebration of the very essence of what it is to be a feline, and a role model for all catkind. To him, we say, "Ack."

CATBERT

Catbert appears in the comic strip *Dilbert*. He works in the same office as the titular character and is frequently employed to strike fear into the hearts of the low-level workers there. He is portrayed as an evil genius, so kudos to creator Scott Adams for getting the genius part right. However, the idea of a cat working beneath a human in a corporation is absurd. If a cat was to work for a human company, it would certainly be at the top. Second, the cat wears spectacles. Right. Third, you never see Catbert taking a nap. He couldn't possibly have the energy to conduct business without taking numerous restorative respites. While it's good to see a cat in a position of power, it is only through assuming the trappings of humans that he gets ahead in the business world. *Dilbert* is apparently very popular, but would probably be more so if Catbert appeared more frequently.

BUCKY KATT

The star of *Get Fuzzy*, silly Siamese Bucky Katt has the ambivalent attitude cats of all stripes can look to for guidance. Bucky is constantly frustrated by his roommate dog, Satchel, and his person, Rob, merely because they do not appreciate the fact that he acts in accordance with common cat sense. Although he is one of three primary characters, Bucky is clearly the hero of the strip, as most of the action is the result of his antics. Despite this, the strip could easily be improved with less cross-species talking and more hissing. Further, Bucky's "in your face" attitude is played more for laughs than serious drama, and that reinforces a certain grotesque caricature of cats that many humans hold.

MOOCH

What's to like about a cat who is written with a speech impediment? A whole lot. Mooch, the best thing about the poorly named strip *Mutts,* is a very calm, insightful cat who is a pillar of zen in a chaotic world. Even though his best friend is a dog, Mooch accurately and positively depicts the best things in life: knocking things off of shelves, napping, and watching life go by. Equally important, Mooch is cute as a kitten, which makes even his least admirable traits enjoyable.

What's in There?

Cats have a thirst for knowledge and an innate curiosity about the world around us. We want to know how humans make the water flow in the sink like that. We crave insight as to why anyone thinks we're fooled by fake mousies, but at the same time, we wonder why we are still drawn to chase them. We yearn to find out what's in the bag that got set down just a second ago. In fact, if we don't find those things out, *right now,* it will simply make us crazy. CRAZY WITH CURIOSITY!

As a feline trait, curiosity is second to none. A cat would turn her attention from a deaf mouse with a limp if she could find out what that bouncing light on the wall is, yet this curiosity is often thwarted by the very humans who purport to care for us.

Our people's grotesque size and opposable thumbs give them easy access, allowing them to deftly open doors and look atop the tallest cupboards. If that is the case, then why do they pull out all stops when it comes to keeping us from having our just peeks? We are shooed, scooted, and scrammed away at every opportunity. Would it kill them to give us one little look-see? Since they don't want us in those places, it *has* to be good!

So what's in those tantalizing spots? After our own exhaustive research and enormous amounts of wild speculation, we have found the answers. This doesn't mean you shouldn't take the opportunity to verify our findings yourself. Poke, peek, and send in your observations if they conflict with the ones contained herein.

THE CUPBOARD UNDER THE SINK

One would think that this spot is a breeze to get into. Nothing but a flimsy piece of wood separates us from this spot. Yet a cat can spend hours trying to work the door open, trying time and time again, only to come up empty-pawed in the end. Curse the wretched being who installed these doors!

So What's in There?

The next time you see your person reaching into the cupboard, take note of what she does. Sometimes she might scrape the contents of a plate or throw an old newspaper under there. Other times she may remove a brightly colored bottle or can. By using a cat's impeccable abilities of deduction, it is obvious that the cupboard houses a little factory in which raw materials are converted into household cleaning products.

THE MEDICINE CABINET

To look at it, you wouldn't think there was much to the medicine cabinet. In fact, the most interesting thing about it is the mirror, where you can see how ravishing you are. In the morning, however, when your person is getting ready to leave the house, she grabs the mirror and pulls it open, revealing a hollow space filled with things you are dying to check out. Only you can't, because any attempt to get up there gets you tossed to the floor. It's not medicine being kept in this so-called "medicine cabinet." What's the big secret?

So What's in There?

Think about how your person looks in the morning when she gets up or when she spends all day sitting around the house in her pajamas, watching movies on cable. Notice how different she appears when she's going out. Her eyes look bigger, her lashes look like whiskers, and her cheeks look like she actually gets sun instead of staying inside, staring at a computer all day. The reason your person spends so much time digging through the medicine cabinet in the morning is that she keeps a disguise in there. But why would your person need a disguise? Our best guess is that she is a criminal on the run from the law, making you an accomplice to a fugitive. How exciting!

UNDER THE BLANKETS

Whenever your person is making the bed, she chases you away instead of allowing you to sprawl out and get covered by the sheet. The rare occasion when a cat sneaks in while her person is in bed reveals nothing, save a pleasant feeling of being surrounded by warmth. Yet this does not mean that there's not something present when your person is away. Something dangerous? Perhaps. But cats thrive on danger, and we must see for ourselves what lies on the other side of the blanket.

So What's in There?

It's not so much what's on *our* side of the blankets as what's on the *other* side of the blankets. Most cats agree that when we are under the blankets, a monster is on the outside. For this reason, you should practice extreme caution. Lie very still. If something on the other side moves, pounce! Or pounce as well as you can when you're covered with blankets. Then, quickly wiggle free and have a look. If there's no monster there, you have scared it away. Good job!

NOTE: Sometimes, when you are on top of the blankets, something might move beneath them. That could be a monster as well, and may pose a danger to your person, who is sleeping peacefully in there. Attack with extreme prejudice.

THE TOOL CHEST

This can come in many shapes, colors, and sizes, but it always has a handle on the top and makes a lot of noise when it moves. How could such a flimsy box hold so much racket? And why do people close it right as your nose is about to get in there? Foiled again!

So What's in There?

These things are actually miniature orchestra pits for street musicians. Most of the time the occupants are asleep. That's why it's usually so quiet. But as soon as it is picked up, the musicians wake up to play and start to tune their instruments. They can't afford real instruments, so they just bang on whatever scraps get thrown in there. If granted access, we could teach them some grand old cat songs like mom used to sing. So let us in there, already!

THE UTILITY CLOSET

This is a door, just like every other door in the house, with one exception: It's almost always closed. Every once in a while, your person pulls it open, really quick like, so there's not even time to run in and check it out for yourself. There's just a rattling noise and darkness. Instead of being scary, though, it's weirdly inviting.

So What's in There?

After ruling out ghosts, monkeys, dirigibles, murderers, and robot dogs, we are left with one alternative: That door leads to a parallel dimension that is filled with everything a cat's heart could desire. Treats grow on trees, and the trees are themselves made of pork loin. There are windows everywhere and the sun is always shining through them. Butterflies are there to be chased from flower to flower, and the ground is just the right softness and temperature for napping. This is why it is *imperative* that you get in there. Call us once you do and keep the door open for us. We readily admit that this hypothesis could be wrong and the closet could just be a place to keep brooms. Either way, it's extremely interesting, and you *have to* let us know.

Hunting Wild Game

As you now know, birds, bugs, and mice make thoughtful gifts, but even if you don't have time to visit the dead vermin aisle at the local Hallmark store, it's still possible to hunt for wild game in and around your own home. Hunting is about tradition. It's about respecting your quarry because you know it put up a good fight. It's about feeling proud to use all the deadly features the cat gods gave you. With your razor-sharp teeth, explosive speed, and stealthy ambush abilities, you are your own perfect weapon.

When it comes to what to hunt, though, the choices can seem overwhelming. Every type of animal needs to be hunted differently. If you're going out on your first pursuit, these targets should get you started on the right foot. Good hunting!

Spiders: Hunting wild game is important because as cats, we have a responsibility to maintain nature's balance. Spiders upset that balance by hunting the same things we do, causing prey populations to drop out of our favor. For that reason, it's necessary to take down these rivals so our future kills don't end up in their sticky traps. Don't try to imitate their hunting style, though. Your poo doesn't make a web nearly as well as the stuff that comes out of a spider. The ground game is where you make your move. Stalk corners of your house—that's where they tend to land after unhooking their invisible bungee cords. When pouncing, aim for the body. Too many otherwise fine hunting cats have nabbed a spider by one of its legs, only to see the arachnid escape using its other seven.

Bumblebees: Bumblebee season runs May through August. You should find some good hunting spots in and around the flower garden. It's a dangerous pursuit, to be sure, but that's part of the excitement. Going toe-to-toe with a species that has a built-in dagger offers a unique challenge for even the most skilled hunter. If you're up for getting a little dirty, construct a bee-blind by covering yourself in dirt beside some blooming sunflowers. When a bumblebee settles down to pollinate, burst out of the ground and take the fat buzzer down!

Fruit Flies: Fruit flies are small game that are a hoot to hunt. Since they are harmless and not too bright, they're also a great starter bug for your kittens. All it takes to get a swarm of these little ding-a-lings to show up is a piece of gross, mushy banana bait. Don't pounce when the first few appear. Instead, be patient and get up to high ground, like the top of a spice rack. The general rule is to wait until between fifteen and four hundred descend upon the fruit before dive-bombing the whole lot of them. Pin down as many as you can, but don't fret if a few get away. The survivors will just breed another swarm for you to hunt.

Mice: Despite what you may have heard, mice aren't usually blind, so you've got to trick one of these sly rodents into thinking it's safe to emerge from whatever wall it inhabits. To bag a big eight-whisker buck, stick to a corner of the room and don't move one bit. Good mousers have to stay absolutely still. Don't blink your eyes, don't flick your tail, don't wiggle your whiskers. Blend into your environment—really become a bump on the carpet. When the mouse appears, wait until it clears the wall, then swoop in for the kill. There are many ways to attack, but the one popularized by Towser, who holds the world record, with 28,999 kills, is to pin the mouse down and then slap slap slap slap slap!

Towser—The Greatest Mouser on Earth

Ants: Like fruit flies, ants tend to congregate around exposed food, but the difference is, these guys go for the food you're actually interested in, and they have the freakish strength to carry it away! Forget the spirit of the hunt and just decimate the herd. Don't be shy when it comes to the number you take down. It's either them or your food. Make a choice, kitties. If you see one of them carrying off a wounded comrade, show no mercy. This is a battle for chow we're talking about.

Birds: Birding is probably the roughest type of hunting, but there's nothing quite like showing flying creatures that even though we may be land-dwellers, cats rule the sky. A bird-free backyard has many advantages. Not only will your person stop wasting money on feeders and birdhouses—money that, by right, should be spent on food for you—but also your sleep will no longer be interrupted by insufferable tweets and chirps. With birding, you have to trust your natural feather radar. When your teeth start to chatter, you'll know a bird is within range. Either streak up a tree and snatch a bird fresh from the nest, or make the target come to you by setting up a trap in a window. Drop some seed on a sill and lift the pane so it thinks it's getting a free meal. When the bird is within a few feet, drop the window and brace yourself for an awesome crash!

Seventeen-Year Locusts: The scarcity of the seventeen-year locust makes it a highly sought-after prize for any wild game hunter. Also, they screech like the dickens and killing them is the only way anybody has figured out how to shut them up. Make sure to respect the four-locust limit so that future generations can experience the thrill of this rare hunt. If you should ever get the chance to eat this yummy quarry, we highly recommend that you consume it right after the kill. The locust's natural juices will rush out and you'll know instantly why some hunters spend their whole lives on the trail of these bugs.

Kitty Litter, Explained

From the moment you saw that box its purpose was clear. You hopped in, did your business, and buried the result.

Why is that? How come we know exactly where to go to the bathroom? Here's where you'll find the answers to that and other questions.

Q: Where does kitty litter come from?

A: That's an easy one. It comes from places like this:

Q: What is it made of?

A: Composition can vary from simple clay for conventional litter to clumping litter, which is often calcium bentonite fused with quartz or diatomaceous earth.

Q: Why do I bury my business with it?

A: That is due to residual instincts from your wild, feral ancestors who had to be extremely conscious and careful

about predators. They were constantly in danger of being attacked and took precautions to ensure the scent of their waste did not give away their location. By burying the waste they increased the chance of remaining undetected. You are simply emulating the same process, and simultaneously having a little fun by kicking stuff all over the place.

Q: **How come sometimes I like to really jet out of there when finished?**

A: Again, residual instinct. Your ancestors were most vulnerable when going to the bathroom and didn't like to dally after finishing—that would have given predators more time to find them. They took off running like their life depended on it, which it sometimes did. You don't have the same concerns, but why hang around in that dingy box when there's better stuff to do upstairs?

Q: **When should I start acting up to get the litter changed?**

A: Some cats simply can't stand to use a litter box that isn't cleaned daily. If that describes you, then protest by going in other places. The downside to this approach is that going outside the box takes the burying out of it and can make your person *really* mad. Other cats don't care much and will

climb a mountain of old litter if necessary. Ultimately this question boils down to a matter of personal preference; it's totally up to you.

Q: Which kitty litter smells the best?

A: That stuff that smells like pine, it's no contest.

Q: Why do humans seem annoyed when you jump in the litter right after they've scooped it?

A: Humans are selfish. They have a great time playing in the litter and then expect you not to use it as intended. You'd think they'd have better things to do and better places to do it than where you go to the bathroom.

Q: Is it true that when humans flush cat litter down the toilet the possibility exists that a parasite, *Toxoplasma gondii,* **could be present in our feces, survive conventional sewage treatment, and make it out to sea, causing fatal infections in marine mammals such as whales, porpoises, and sea otters?**

A: Not our problem, but yes.

Q: Are there cats who don't use litter and actually go where humans go?

A: Yes. There are cats who will, over time, submit to using a human-style toilet.

Q: Are they for real?

A: They are highly regarded by humans, who fancy them as a more highly evolved feline. However, no, these cats are not for real, they're tools.

Q: Is it acceptable to track litter around where you live?

A: Sure. You may want to minimize that, though, by jumping on your person's bed for a nap after being in the litter box. That way you're not depositing it in so many different places.

About the only thing we haven't touched on is what our people

do with the litter they put in little baggies that come from the grocery store. The answer is that most of the estimated two million tons, or approximately 100,000 truckloads, will end up in a landfill. This is too bad, because there is such a thing as biodegradable litter. It is a little more expensive but lasts longer and doesn't require as much to do the job. Don't count on them changing over anytime soon, though. Like us, humans don't give a lot of thought to waste disposal. It's just easier to bury the stuff and forget about it.

For Black Cats—Making the Most of Superstition

❧

What is it about humans and superstitions? They toss perfectly good salt over their shoulders, eschew the quickest path if it goes under a ladder, and descend into full-on panic after breaking a mirror. When it comes to black cats, humans the world over have no end to their silly hang-ups. Some revere black cats as a symbol of fortune and health, others fear black cats as a symbol of evil and death. Trek through the streets of India and passersby might sooner dash into a cobra-filled alley than cross your path; but take a tour of the Scottish Highlands and locals might want to snatch you up and put you on their porches for good luck.

All of this nonsense has been going on for a long time. A black cat in the American colonies during the seventeenth century had to constantly run for her life, especially if her person wore a pointy black hat and had warts on her nose. On the other hand, a jet-black kitty chilling out in a cabaret in nineteenth-century Paris was the coolest bohemian on the block.

Humans don't seem to realize that black cats are no different than regular cats, so sassy sables out there might as well take advantage of their unique pigmentation.

Clear the Streets! In many Western countries, people have a neurotic compulsion to steer clear of coal-colored cats. This behavior is obviously ridiculous, but rather than be offended by it, instead learn to harness your power over these 'fraidy humans. When strolling outside, run full speed and cut back and forth so fast that no matter where the humans are, none of them feel safe from your "black magic." Use this tac-

tic at malls, amusement parks, big city sidewalks, or wherever you think a path is too crowded for your liking. This trick works especially well around Halloween, when little humans clog the streets looking for free candy. Besides the sheer joy of watching humans scramble out of your way, it's really nice not to go through the hassle of finding a costume.

Get a Change of Scenery Some Europeans, especially Germans and Italians, hold the belief that a black cat on a bed means impending death for the human who sleeps in it. This belief is, of course, pure poppycock, but if you've been hoping to play with that big green Pilates ball over at your person's best friend's place, your black fur could be the key. Just hop up on your person's mattress and stare for a good long while. Pretty soon she'll start freaking out and getting her final affairs in order, which includes giving you to her best friend. Don't worry about becoming

homesick. It shouldn't take too long for your person to realize she's completely fine, and once she does, you'll be welcomed back with open arms. The timing should work out well, since you'll probably puncture the exercise ball right away and realize that was pretty much the only fun thing in the house.

Get a Free Cruise Seafarers have long believed that having a black cat on board a ship brings calm seas and fair winds. Haven't these sailors ever heard of tracking nimbostratus and cumulonimbus clouds? Apparently not, but as long as they insist upon using black cats as their lucky

For Black Cats—Making the Most of Superstition

meteorologists, you might as well snag a free trip to the Caribbean out of it. According to captains' lore, all you have to do to be taken aboard is run in front of a sailor as he makes his way down a dock. Don't worry about walking the plank if your ship is overtaken by pirates. Throwing a cat overboard is considered a major violation of maritime conduct and is said to cause fierce storms and choppy seas.

Earn Great Riches and Eat Well! The Chinese have varying views on the meaning of black cats. Some believe they are symbols of coming poverty, while others see them as signs of imminent financial prosperity. If you live indoors, it's a safe bet your person thinks you're of the prosperous ilk, and therefore you can use the superstition to your benefit. Let's say your person plays the Hang Seng Index in Hong Kong. Just scratch the stock symbol of a favorite food company in the morning paper and start meowing. A chain of economic events will soon follow. Your person buys up shares of the company, the stock skyrockets, and soon servings of Duck à l'Orange from the food producer's new gourmet line are filling your bowl.

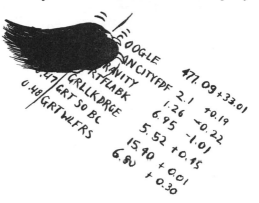

Ruin a Sports Franchise Nothing is quite as frustrating as a human who isn't focused on petting you because he's glued to a stupid televised sporting event. Even sitting in his lap is maddening because of all the springing up to cheer or scream. Black cats can help us all out by doing what one enterprising noir feline did in 1969 during a Cubs–Mets

game at Shea Stadium. The black cat bolted out onto the field and walked ominously around Cubs infielder Ron Santo. Next thing you know, the Cubs blew an eight-game lead in the play-off hunt, and Chicago-area cats finally got the attention they deserved from humans no longer occupied with watching baseball.

Shelf Swat

❖

Knocking things off shelves for sport, more commonly known as the game of shelf swat, was first played in 1835 by Smokey, a Maine Coon living in Bangor. Originally, it consisted of a simple wooden mantle over a fireplace, a small pair of deer antlers, six tin cans, and two beeswax candles, but today it has evolved into a global athletic phenomenon. Luminaries of the game have broken some of humanity's most precious valuables, and in so doing inspired kittens everywhere to do the same. Like all great sports, shelf swat has had its controversies. Many questioned '90s-era champion shelf-swatter Sprinkles after he somehow knocked off a petrified dinosaur bone four times his own weight. However, it is undeniably the beloved national pastime of our species.

Scoring in shelf swat is awarded based on three criteria: item, choreography, and artistry. Some cats focus on racking up as many points as possible in one category, while others go for a strong average across the board. Since every shelf is different, it's best not to lock yourself into a scoring strategy until it's determined which shelf you'll be playing on.

ITEM

Points in this category are awarded based on monetary value. Some shelf-swatters swear by the strategy of knocking off just a few high-value items, while others try to run up the score based on pushing over a high number of low-value objects. Item lingo can get pretty confusing, so try to learn some basic terms.

Crasher: An object that makes a loud noise when it hits the floor. Item points vary, but these often net big scores in the artistic category. Blintz, who played in the American Shelf-Swat League (later absorbed into the International Shelf-Swatters Association) from 1940 to 1944, was nicknamed "The King of Crash" for his mastery of knocking over items like cowbells, silver teakettles, and coffee cans full of coins.

Illumi-knockoffs: Humans turn these on to brighten up the place. Generally one will bring in 30–50 points, but if the item is really old or has a beer insignia, it could be worth a lot more.

Time-suckers: These are things that humans either read, watch, or listen to. Even though they don't bring in a lot of points on a per-item basis (generally in the range of 13.95 to 23.50), they

often exist in big groups on shelves, so the cumulative score can be huge. Isis, 2006's Rookie of the Year, made her mark on the league by swatting off her person's entire 1,500-piece world-music CD collection in under three minutes.

Breakers: If you've got a breaker on your shelf, it could be a point-scoring bonanza. These objects are often found in the homes of humans called "glass sculpture

collectors," and values can soar in the tens or even hundreds of thousands. Bonus points are awarded for a shatter radius of more than four feet.

CHOREOGRAPHY

The Flick (5 points): The flick is the most basic move, which you must master to become a champion shelf-swatter. Cats who go for speed frequently flick because it knocks a lot off the shelf in a short amount of time. To use the flick, just align your forelimb flush with an object, snap, and pull back quickly. The motion should come naturally, because it's a lot like the movement paws make when you're dreaming.

The Fakey (10 points): This full-body fake-out move can net you some big-time points. First, pass over the object as if you aren't going to knock it over. Then, in a single, fluid motion, push it underneath your body, and leap up

"The Flick"

ing like he wasn't going to knock off an item that his person never was able to catch him, thus explaining why he was never ordered to get down off a shelf.

The Grand Dare (14 points): This move is all about theatricality. Focus on an object the width of the space between your outstretched paws, like a big fancy candle or a Precious Moments figurine. Make sure your person is present and looking at you when executing the move. Place one paw on either side of the item—close enough to smack it, but not making direct contact. Stare directly into the eyes of your person and really build up the suspense over whether or not you'll knock it off the shelf. Then, the second your person gets up to try and grab the item, let it rip. The Russian swat master Masha Leveetsana was renowned for her

into the air. Give the item a real good heave, too, because the farther it goes flying, the more points are allotted. Once you master the move, try adding an aerial flourish to your finishing leap with a vertical spin.

Fourteen-year league veteran Frizzler attributed his unprecedented longevity in the game to frequent use of the fakey. So skilled was Frizzler at pretend-

graceful, dramatic execution of the grand dare, which she once performed with a Fabergé egg from Tsar Alexander III's personal collection.

The Wedgie (20 points): Lesser cats wither away when faced with a shelf packed with items. Pros use the wedgie. You've got to be fearless (some would say nuts) to try it, but in a game of shelf swat, there's no more advanced move. To do it, get on one end of the shelf, hug the wall, and squeeze behind each item so they tip off, one by one, as you pass by. Seems easy, right? Well, that's what every cat says until she's in the tool-shed, trying to squish past a forty-pound bucket of loose nails and finds herself stuck. Kitties, for your own safety, leave this move to the pros.

ARTISTRY

Scoring in this category is based on the human judge's decision, which is made at the moment the object falls off the shelf. Many cats, for obvious reasons, object to letting a human's opinion figure into the score, but every great sport needs an x-factor and shelf swat is no exception. A judge's score can be determined as follows:

1–2 points

3–6 points

7–9 points

10 points!

PENALTIES

There are no penalties in shelf swat, nor are there "losers." As in life, there are just degrees to which a cat wins.

The Legend of the Crazy Cat Lady

The Legend of the Crazy Cat Lady has been told on camping trips for generations. Cats have held their kittens spellbound around the fire with this cautionary tale about the dangers of straying too far from home and snooping in houses where they don't belong. When telling this story yourself, it helps if you make it your own by adding in personal details and insisting that it happened to your cousin or neighbor. By the end, if you tell it well, all the kittens are scared straight, and a little extra flourish will make them all scream!

No one knows where the Crazy Cat Lady lives or how she got to be the Crazy Cat Lady. Some people say she was just a normal lady who lost her mind when someone swindled her out of a great fortune. Other people say she was a lonely woman who thought she loved cats, but what she really loved was the feeling of being needed by cats that couldn't make her understand that they could do just fine without her. Wherever she came from, one thing is for sure: She is crazy and she has a lot of cats.

You wouldn't think that is such a bad thing; but on the contrary, it is worse than you could possibly imagine.

The Crazy Cat Lady lives alone in a small ranch house with two thousand newspapers and almost a hundred cats and only leaves to buy cat litter and cat food. When she does, she bundles herself from head to foot with mismatched scarves and coats and mittens.

If you go to her house, perhaps on a dare, the first thing you notice is the smell. Only it's less a smell than a force of odor that hits you right square in the nose. It smells like almost a hundred cats had one litter box to use, and they've used it all they can. That impression is correct, because one Crazy Cat Lady cannot clean one litter box enough to keep it nice and fresh like the one you have at home.

After you get past the torrid stank, you start to smell the newspapers. It's not a wholly unpleasant odor, but the smell of two thousand newspapers is singular. Normal people would recycle them before they got so musty, or at least stack them in the basement or garage, but the Crazy Cat Lady loves newspapers as much as she thinks she loves cats, so they sit there, smelling, smelling.

Your brain has been so busy processing the smells you barely notice that it's impossible to see anything because the curtains are drawn tight. As your eyes adjust to the dark, you can't make out any shapes. All you see is movement.

At first, you think it's just out of the corner of your eye, but then you realize it's everywhere, all around you. It's the movement of almost a hundred cats in search of a perching spot that isn't already occupied. It's the movement of almost a hundred cats trying to sneak up on one another to pounce on them in play, only to be pounced on themselves. It's the movement of almost a hundred cats scampering and sniffing about for scraps of food they might have missed after being forced to compete with almost ninety-nine other cats for a morsel or kibble that has not yet been consumed.

But it's not just food they're after. If a human visitor enters, the cats will swarm, craving a skritching because there's almost a hundred of them and only one lady with two hands to give them skritches, and unless she has company, which she rarely does because she is crazy, their chins go horribly underskritched.

But you are not a human. You are a cat, and it's much different. They will all swarm on you to sniff you, trying to catch the scent of the outside in your fur, because they have long forgotten what the not-house smells like. They also want to size you up to see if you will be much competition for the food that is just scattered on the floor at feeding time, because it is inconvenient to keep almost a hundred cat dishes clean.

Then you hear her. Her call sounds like "Here, kitty kitty kitty!" or "Oh, how precious!" Even though you're trying to blend in amongst almost a hundred other cats, she spots you immediately and zeroes in. She can tell by the brightness in your eyes that you are not like the others. Before you can react, she swoops in and picks you up under the forelegs, like one would hold a baby human. You can try to struggle, but there's no escaping her grip.

"Oh, you have tags!" she'll say, and for once you are thankful for that horrible collar your person makes you wear. You think it's over, because she has to follow the rule of humans and call the number on your tag. You breathe a sigh of relief, until you feel her dry, cracked fingers fumbling at your neck.

In the blink of an eye, she removes your collar and throws it in the trash. "There. Isn't that better?" she says, but it isn't better. Never has having an unrestricted neck felt so confining. "Now you can live with me and all my babies. Look at you! You have a nose, so I'll call you Button 2."

You try to explain that this makes no sense, that all the cats have noses, that Button 2 isn't your name, that you have some serious concerns about what happened to the first Button, and that you aren't a baby, but a cat that belongs to a very nice uncrazy cat lady who will miss you very much. But she's already gone back into her other room to watch soap operas and yell that the commercials are getting too suggestive. And you fear that you will spend the rest of your life as the Crazy Cat Lady's one hundredth cat.

But just as you've lost all hope the doorbell rings. You climb under the curtain and spy a man dressed all in brown. He's holding a package and a clipboard. The look on his face says he knows what smell lies behind the door, and he's already holding his breath. The Crazy Cat Lady makes her way to the door, shooing all the cats away, but you hide behind an umbrella stand filled with junk mail.

As the door opens, you see your big chance. You summon all your strength and bolt out. Everyone is surprised, but it's too late to stop you. You run as far as you can, leaving behind the sounds of the man in brown apologizing to the Crazy Cat Lady, until you hide under a bush to catch your breath. When you finally get home, it's never felt so good to be inside.

So whatever you do, stay away from strange houses, and never, EVER look in the mirror after midnight and say "Crazy Cat Lady" three times, or she will come and SNATCH YOU!

Felinism

———————— ❧ ————————

Since its late-nineteenth-century inception, the goal of felinism has been to ensure freedom and opportunity across all spheres of cat life. From the right to claws to equal time outdoors, felinism has forced the Western world to examine its attitudes toward cats and their perceived place in society. Felinists are leaders, not followers, of public opinion.

Historically the word "felinism" referred to "the general qualities of felines," and it was not until 1892 that the word, following the French term *féliniste,* was used regularly to describe the advocacy of more rights for cats. Felinism has never enjoyed a truly universal definition, but most scholars agree that it seems to involve two tenets. One seeks to address how cats *ought* to be viewed and treated. The other is a reaction to how cats *are* treated, rebelling against myths created to confine them in an oppressed state. The overall aim of felinism as a movement is to dispel the notion that cats are not the greatest.

As it has progressed, some theorists cite three periods, or waves, of activity.

THE FIRST WAVE OF FELINISM

First-wave felinism refers to a period during the early twentieth century that focused primarily on dispelling the idea that cats are somehow inferior when compared with other animals. Even today, studies show that in arguments of compatibility, cats are still frequently characterized unfavorably and portrayed as aloof, unemotional, and moody.

First-wave felinists were committed to effecting change, but progress would not come easily. Prominent cats of the movement, such as Pants of Cleveland, Ohio, were leaders and dedicated much of their lives to championing the cause. Many hours were spent in laps demonstrating that cats are just as capable of affection as anybody else.

Pants

Despite the fact that species discrimination still exists, the work of first-wave felinists eventually made cats more popular than dogs. Today there are 68 million dogs "owned" in the United States. By comparison, 73 million cats live with people. Cats are simply more popular, and as such, it can be strongly argued that they are better. Five million times better.

THE SECOND WAVE OF FELINISM

Beginning in the 1960s, felinism entered its second wave. Second-wave felinism picked up where the first wave left off, recognizing the strides that were made but further encouraging cats to understand their lives as part of a power structure that ultimately was controlling and insulting.

Felinist Couch

Felinists of the second wave demanded that their autonomous nature be fully acknowledged and respected. This era encouraged cats to confront the implications of how they had been stereotyped and to embrace the belief that they were valuable as more than just companions, or worse, mere pets.

Cats began to reevaluate aspects of their lives that had previously been considered sacrosanct. The idea that cats needed to have doors opened for them was challenged by those who showed that they could easily wedge their paws under a door and open it, *if they so desired.* The second wave of felinism strove to open cats' eyes to possibilities of achievement and advancement long denied them.

This period also saw a marked increase in civil disobedience. In response to the arbitrary discrimination of repeatedly being banned from furniture in the living room, Phyllis, a calico from Boston, Massachusetts, was the first cat to completely cover the couch in her fur. She also would not sleep a wink in the demeaning "cat bed" that her person put in the corner. Throughout the United States, felinists followed Phyllis's example and began shedding all over couches.

THE THIRD WAVE OF FELINISM

Third-wave felinists are those who have experienced a different life than older cats and feel that it sets them apart. These cats benefited from the work of cats before them but came of age in a frenzied world where it was necessary to juggle a person, sleep, and work.

Third-wavers seek to challenge the second wave's ideas about what constitutes the idealized life of a cat. Their contention is that the second wave demeans those who are perfectly happy sleeping in a barn, raising kittens, or eating mice.

Stan the Man, a tabby from New Orleans, Louisiana, is a third-wave felinist who enjoys traditional cat pursuits, like spending time in the sun, but equally appreciates nontraditional activities like getting into the bathtub as the water is draining out.

Standing in the warm water, Stan the Man doesn't care what anybody thinks. He's all-the-way happy doing what he wants, and that's what he'd like for all felinists. By purring to successes of the past while staring at the future, third-wave felinists continue to fight for a total emancipation of the cat.

Stan the Man

An Illustrated Guide to Napping

Nothing caps off a solid day of doing nothing quite like a good nap. Also, nothing starts off a day of doing nothing like a nap. And there's really nothing better than a nap to help you break up a busy afternoon, relax after an uneventful evening, or wind down from a hectic weekend of relaxing and taking naps.

Without a doubt, napping is one of our favorite activities. It's enjoyed by cats young and old, and it isn't likely to go out of style anytime soon. Surveys show that the popularity of napping among cats ages 18 to 34 months has never been higher.

Humans enjoy making fun of our propensity for slumber, but the fact is, the smarter and more efficient cat brain requires more downtime than its human counterpart. It's obvious when you look at humans that they don't get enough sleep. They have terrible balance, bump into things in the dark, and can't pounce worth a dime.

Most humans also think all naps are just about the same. Cats know nothing could be further from the truth. There are hundreds of varieties of naps, and a proper time and place for each. Would you ever try to doze in a closet? Of course not. That's the place to go for a little shut-eye. And who would take a snooze right after din-din? Certainly not you! That's the time to catch some z's. Here's a guide to some of our favorite napping styles, to help make sure you choose the right one.

Snooze: Those three to four hours between lunch and dinner in the mid-afternoon are the perfect time for a snooze. The snooze is the uncontested King of Naps and is best enjoyed on a blanket-covered lap. It's even better if your person is snoozing

Snoozing

beneath you. The snooze is a perennial favorite of the rock 'n' roll cat who loves to play all day and party all night. You wake up feeling refreshed and ready to eat and bash into things. More things.

Doze: If you've ever been in a hurry to nap but didn't have time for a snooze, you've probably chosen a doze. Dozing off is fulfill-ing at any time of day, but especially during news programs, political round-table discussions, and soap operas. The classic doze incorporates quick bursts of deep restfulness punctuated by an occasional meow, just to check in with your person or other feline roomies. That way, if something interesting is happening, you can get up and investigate. Though most cats believe a doze can be interrupted any number of times without diluting the quality of the dozing, some cats think three interruptions is too many. If this occurs, just get up and nibble on a little something before trying a different nap style.

Resting: A rest is a wonderful starter nap and makes a great prelude to a doze. Ideally you'll

Dozing

Resting

enjoy resting best in the evening, on the bed while your person is reading a steamy paperback romance or watching a gripping medical drama. A true rest includes vigorous purring, intense snuggling, and at least four full body repositionings on your human's head, face, chest, and stomach.

Catching Some Z's: Z's are a great pick-me-up and the perfect way to rest worn-out paws after painstakingly unraveling a handmade shawl. Catch some lying in the "sun spot" on top of the loveseat or, alternately, the warm space on top of the television. Snoring is encouraged during this fifteen-to-twenty-minute restorative. The most widely photographed nap in the canon.

Catnapping

Catnap: This classic, all-purpose nap works wonders on all the major napping muscles. It can be taken whenever and wherever you like, and lasts exactly as long as you please. Just plop yourself right down wherever you are and drift off into slumber. You'll sleep most soundly when positioned inconveniently. Aim to stretch out across the lap of someone who has to relieve themselves, or spread out over the receipts at tax time.

Catching some z's

"The Siesta"

Siesta: The cat who had a little too much fun running up and down the stairs the night before will often choose a refreshing siesta to recharge. The siesta is a festive slumber that *gatitos* have been taking for centuries, and there's no better way to say *buenas noches.*

Shut-eye: Cats in the armed forces have been getting a little shut-eye whenever they could since way back in the days of the Revolutionary War. It is believed that Paul Revere's cat, Breetches, perfected the style when she was supposed to be on lookout for the British. Nowadays, it makes no difference whether you're stationed on an aircraft carrier or in a kitty carrier. You can sneak in a little shut-eye no matter where you're deployed. Take it whenever you can get it.

Getting some shut-eye

Extraordinary Cats in History—Part II

—✿—

ISAAC NEWTON'S CATS

Between his groundbreaking astronomical findings, discovering the laws of gravity, and dividing the visible light spectrum, Sir Isaac Newton wasted a lot of people's time. Many contend that the one innovation of any real use, the kitty door, is not even his to claim. In fact, Charles R. Gibson notes in his *Stories of Great Scientists* that "It would be difficult to realize Newton taking care of a dog or a cat, he was so unmindful of himself."

In our estimation, Gibson was half right. After examining the historical record, we have reached our own theory: Newton did have cats, as evidenced by the kitty doors on his home, but there is no way that bumbling nerd took proper care of them. Thus, the logical conclusion is that Newton's cats, and not Newton, invented the kitty door, since the device would have enabled the cats to enjoy the outdoors whenever they pleased without having to rely on their so-called "genius" of a person.

Furthermore, we believe we have discovered how the landmark invention came into being: On a pleasant English afternoon in the late seventeenth century, Newton was toiling away on something or other that only sophomore physics majors care about when his cat and her kitten informed him that they wanted to sunbathe and that he should open the front door for them posthaste. Ever the absentminded professor, he thoughtlessly ignored his cats, so they set their keen intellects to finding a solution for themselves.

Newton's cats went straight for their Eukittyian math textbook, cracked it open, studied for nineteen seconds, became distracted by a hovering beetle, licked each other, ripped up some document called "An

Astounding New Law of Physics Proving Humans Can Fly on Their Own," took a nap, and then jotted down this landmark equation:

$$039.335y \sum Nx \pm \sqrt{(3\pi + H)} \Big/ \big\| (3\lambda + W) \big\|$$

Simply put, it states that a rectangular opening roughly three centimeters larger than the height and width of a cat provides the most efficient means of temporary domestic escape. Newton's kitten posited that a flap affixed to the top of the hole would keep out both unwanted precipitation and squirrels too dumb to figure out how to go through it.

Newton's cat and kitten considered building the hole in the door themselves, but then recalled every physicist's duty to follow the path of least resistance. In this case, that meant sharing the equation with Newton so that he'd build the door for them. Upon reviewing their findings, Newton promptly built a hole for his cat, and a smaller one for her kitten. Then, with a few tweaks of the equation—carrying the three, substituting a variable, and changing the whole thing completely—he developed the Generalized Binomial Theorem.

GIN-GIN, CONQUEROR OF THE SEATTLE SCRATCHING POST

It was the year 2000 and Seattle residents were in a bit of a funk. Grunge music was dead, the whole world was co-opting the hometown coffee brew, and the dot-com good times were almost at an end. Cats in the Northwest knew they needed an awesome achievement to make everybody forget their troubles, if only momentarily. After a quick brainstorming session, they decided that the sight of a Washingtonian feline reaching the giant scratching post at the top of the Seattle Space Needle would be just the thing to turn the city's spirits around. The Space Needle stood tall over the Emerald City, beckoning intrepid climbers to scale its heights, but what cat would answer the call?

Gin-Gin, a Burmese living in the Seattle suburb of Bothell, decided to take up the challenge. She practiced for months, spending each day climbing pine trees and telephone poles. Many safety-conscious supporters had pushed her to use equipment—harnesses, ropes, a helmet—but she knew that the achievement would be hollow if it wasn't a free climb.

In the early-morning hours of October 4, she set out to begin her glorious ascent, but before reaching the first base camp, destiny tested Gin-Gin's mettle. As she clung to the eighth rivet, a group of patchouli-scented teens formed a hacky-sack circle below and started kicking. Gin-Gin was pelted several times by the rainbow-colored footbag, but finally climbed above the barrage and left the floppy-haired twerps behind. The morning ascent went well, as the weather was cooperative, and Gin-Gin was able to stop at 230 feet to rest and lick out some of the ground turkey bits she had packed in her paws.

At the 450-foot mark, unfortunately, things took a turn toward the dramatic. In planning her climb, Gin-Gin had failed to consider the tempting smells emanating from SkyCity, the revolving restaurant that stood between her and the tippy-top, and now she was paying for that oversight.

The aroma of the Pacific Northwest's finest king salmon filled her nostrils, beckoning her to abandon the dream of scratching Seattle's highest post. Through the observation deck windows sat the beautifully glazed fillets—those pink delicacies calling Gin-Gin away from her glorious quest. Still, she was a fearless, resourceful kitty—imbued from birth with the heart of a trailblazer. Shaking off the scent, Gin-Gin spotted a window-cleaning crew working on the south face of the observation deck. Without making a sound, she snuck up to the suspended window-cleaning platform, swiped a safety carabiner, and clipped it onto her nose.

The intoxicating fish smell no longer a distraction, Gin-Gin resumed her climb, against all the odds, and headed for the final leg of the ascent.

The winds picked up, the air thinned out, but nothing could stop Gin-Gin now. As the Pacific sky began to dim, Gin-Gin reached the top of the Space Needle and, with a chest full of pride, clawed that behemoth scratching spire in a heroic triumph for both the cats and the people of Seattle.

Catnip

The chapter you are about to read may be startling, particularly to young kittens, but the truth we are about to reveal emphasizes the danger that this botanical enemy poses to catkind. Its smell is alluring, even sweet, but be forewarned: If you think it won't lead to sadness and tears, you're only fooling yourself. This scourge, this catnip, can only lead down a primrose path to destruction, and if you're not careful, you may be the one lazily rolling down that path.

Catnip pushers are shrewd. They may be somebody you know. You can be sitting around, minding your own business when they bring a little baggie home from their "connection" at the pet store. They may even grow it themselves in the backyard. Never mind that this leafy menace ruins lives all around the globe. All they know is that it makes cats act "funny." They don't care that all it takes is one "hit" and a cat is hooked. No, the pusher just wants to ply you with some "good stuff" for her own twisted amusement.

Sure, it tastes good when you chew it, and it feels good, too. For a while, anyway. Then you will be seized by the uncontrollable urge to roll, as if in a trance. Before you know it, you'll be on the floor, rolling in the catnip, getting it caught in your beautiful fur.

Suddenly, nothing seems to matter. Space and time expand. Paws suddenly become more interesting, and you really notice how furry your fur is. Music you never liked before is now "blowing your mind." You try to get up and find that it's more difficult than you remember. You decide it would be better just to stay where you are and roll around on the ground for a while longer.

Then, it all starts to go bad. The feeling of euphoria gives way to acute paranoia. Everyone is trying to get you, even your favorite toy. Your interest in food and petting wanes. You'll try to take refuge in your usual hiding places, but find that there is no place to hide from your own mind. After a few hours of thinking the nightmare will never end, it finally fades, and you think you're back to normal. You promise yourself—never again.

Then the craving starts. You've heard the stories about cats who get hooked, but that's not you. You just want to try some of that sweet, sweet catnip one more time. You can quit any time you want. But as soon as the pusher shows up and sprinkles more catnip on your scratching post, you lose control. You promise yourself that this will definitely be the last time, that you won't become "one of those cats." Days roll by, then weeks. Before you know it, the catnip is all gone, and your person doesn't seem to understand that she needs to go back to that pet store and buy more. NOW!

Nothing matters but getting more catnip. It's all you think about. You crawl around the carpet to see if there's any that you missed. You dig around in your food dish, searching for any there. You'll try to sneak out of the house to look for some growing in the backyard. Never mind that there's a foot of snow on the ground and you aren't allowed outside. There's a monkey on your back, and catnip is the only way to make it stop its hideous screeching.

Before you know it, all your toys will be chewed up beyond recognition because you're sure there has to be more catnip in them. You try to break into your person's cupboards to see if she's holding out on you. Endless days and sleepless nights will be spent dreaming of that next batch. You're a changed cat, and rue the day you ever tried that horrible catnip.

We know what you're thinking. That will never happen to me. But this scenario is based on the true stories of former catnip addicts. They got away from it with their lives. You might not be so lucky. Remember, if someone approaches you with some catnip, just say meow and keep walking. If it's too late for that, you *can* quit the horrible habit—but you can't do it alone. There are plenty of 12-step organizations out there that can help you kick the habit. Just take it one day at a time, and eventually you will be a stronger cat.

Once you're clean, forever avoid the lure of the weed with roots in hell. Because the dread catnip may be reaching forth next for your kittens . . . or *yours* . . . or YOURS!

Organizing an Effective Secret Mission

If you live in a home with several other feline friends, you have the opportunity to carry out one of the most devious activities in the whole cat universe: executing secret missions. Secret missions can include food-pantry incursions, head-of-household coups, and pest assassinations. Solo kitties can take on any one of these missions by themselves, but cats who work together often achieve more effective, more efficient results. Assigning specific operational roles is important to any secret mission, so decide ahead of time which cat best suits the duties listed below. To help in your planning, let's examine the dynamics of a common secret mission: getting up on the dinner table to explore and pilfer the contents of shopping bags.

Mission Accomplished

The Mastermind: Plotting any kind of operation takes time and attention to detail. The mastermind sets the mission objective and coordinates the efforts of all the other cats to achieve it. This cat is also responsible for assessing whether or not the goal of the mission is worth the risk of being locked in the basement, which it usually is. At the end of the mission, the mastermind will be the cat purring on top of the dinner table and divvying up the treasure inside the shopping bags as she sees fit.

The Cuddler: This is the cat who can make a human coo with the mere brush of her tail. She knows how to use her adorable peepers, cute little soft paws, and overall irresistible cuddliness to get what she wants. Need to distract your person while the rest of the squad makes off with the cheddar? Then the cuddler is your pussycat. For the dinner table raid, the cuddler should assume a dedicated position firmly in the lap of your person. If there are more than four shopping bags to investigate, the cuddler will have to keep your person occupied with affection for at least a solid hour.

The Sentinel: This job should be assigned to the cat in your crew who always perches at the top of the bookcase. The sentinel is responsible for staying elevated, maintaining sight lines, and alerting cats in the field to any sign of danger. Make sure your sentinel isn't the quiet type. If she catches sight of an approaching human—or the mouse that's been getting into your Meow Mix Seafood Medley—she had better

be able to caterwaul like a ban-shee. In addition, the sentinel must have preternatural vision. Being able to see a baseball on a lawn three miles away in the pitch black of night is the mini-mum requirement for all cats, so the sentinel should be able to see at least double that distance. If you plan to attack the dinner table while the humans are out, station your sentinel at the high-est window in the house, or per-haps even on the roof.

The Weapons Expert: With spikes for teeth and knives for claws, the weapons expert is the cat best equipped to do the dirty work. Of course, this sly kitty is responsible for slicing open even the supposedly impenetrable food pouches, but she can also help out if you need to cut com-munication hard lines or disable

motion sensors. When making your foray into dinner table terri-tory, the weapons expert should assist the mastermind by shred-ding the shopping bags open for faster plundering.

The Bag-Cat: The bag-cat is the muscle who isn't afraid of a little heavy lifting. Often tipping the scales at around fourteen pounds, bag-cats aren't the most inconspicuous felines, but they make up in strength what they lack in stealth. If your operation involves dragging away a bulk-sized tube of Jimmy Dean

BAG-CAT

sausage or knocking over a big clay flowerpot that blocks a favorite view, you'll need one of these bruisers. Any leftovers on the table should be pushed over the side by the mastermind, at which point the bag-cat transports the morsels to an undisclosed rendezvous point for safe consumption.

The Whisker Specialist: Your whisker specialist is responsible for GPS analysis and mapping the route of the mission. Using her finely tuned facial hairs, she evaluates spatial proportions and determines whether it is safe to infiltrate a vase, squeeze through a crack under a door, or scale a chimney. Her whiskers can also pick up on changes in wind patterns caused by the layout of objects in a room, making her essential to navigating around potentially unstable climbing structures.

The Electronics Whiz: Any successful dinner table mission needs a crack electronics whiz. The whiz in your group is the one who spends her days batting computer screens or click-clacking all over keyboards. These tech goddesses keep their methods to themselves, but we're pretty sure that spending all of their time in front of the computer allows them to do things like hack into FDA servers to order a recall of nasty food brands. Chances are that during the dinner table mission, the electronics whiz won't move from your person's laptop. Don't disturb her. She's doing her thing, whatever it is.

WHISKER SPECIALIST

ELECTRONICS WHIZ

Egypt: The Land We Once Ruled

Felines have influenced countless religions and societies throughout the ages. The pages of history are rife with displays of gratitude from those who benefited from their generous wisdom. Nowhere is this more evident than in Egypt, a kingdom that produced its greatest triumphs when ruled by cats.

Egyptian civilization was plagued with hordes of grain-stealing rats, and early attempts to control them were largely unsuccessful.

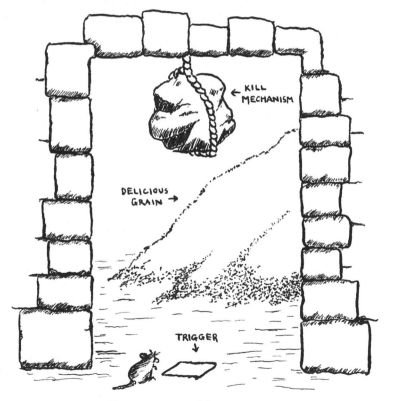

Early Egyptian Mousetrap

To make matters worse, cobras were swarming the kingdom. Egyptians eventually realized that no amount of social pressure would stop them from biting people.

The Egyptians finally turned to cats for help.

Being well acquainted with both adversaries, cats quickly began to kill rats and send snakes packing. As word spread of their amazing success and obvious intelligence, cats were invited to join the human population in ever-growing numbers.

Reverence soon followed acceptance and cats began to be worshipped, rising to the highest levels of Egyptian religion. Artisans who fashioned sculptures and amulets of Bast, a goddess who was originally thought to have looked like a crabby, scary-breasted lion that walked on two legs, changed their rendering. After being suitably impressed by the actions and deeds of cats, they began depicting Bast as a dignified tabby, reflecting grace and poise.

EEEEK!

Better

As a result of their ascension, cats also began to attain prestigious political positions. Ruling cats lived in lavish palaces, and the killing of any feline became a capital offense. Archaeologists have uncovered many pieces of Egyptian artwork that chronicle the everyday life of a ruling cat.

Ruling cats kept humans called pharaohs as advisers. Together cats and pharaohs ushered in cultural achievements of lasting significance.

THE PYRAMIDS

Meo-ow-tep was the first of many great cat rulers to build a pyramid. The plan was to build the greatest perch the world had ever seen. Meo-ow-tep saw such a perch during a vision. It was in the form of a pyramid, and the biggest cat in the world rested on top.

A pyramid was an ideal shape to represent the perfect perch. At the top there was room for only one cat to sit. There could be no better vantage point to survey all that had been conquered than from the apex of a grand pyramid.

Meo-ow-tep's Vision

Unfortunately Meo-ow-tep's vision was never realized. Human error, insubordination, and general laziness all conspired to undermine the project. The pyramids of subsequent cat rulers tragically found the same fate, with the pharaohs unable to execute the elegant plans of their cat rulers. However, even the unfinished pyramids stand as testament to the abilities of those like Meo-ow-tep, who conceived of them.

THE SPHINX

It is unknown precisely which cat ruler built a massive Sphinx guarding the pyramids at Giza. Most archaeologists attribute it to Scramses, who had a pharaoh named Khafre. The Sphinx is a giant cat-body carving, over 200 feet long and 65 feet high, with paws measuring 50 feet in length. Like many cat rulers who undertook such massive projects, Scramses did not live to see its completion, and it is widely thought that Khafre must have finished supervising the construction, heretically substituting his own face for that of Scramses on the head of the Sphinx.

MUMMIFICATION

The practice of wrapping a body in strips of linen was first introduced to the Egyptians by cats. Legend has it that when a cat was observed transforming itself into a mummy, humans sought to honor it by adopting the practice for their own burial rituals.

Many cat rulers had themselves permanently mummified for their eternal nap, occasionally allowing a decent pharaoh to be buried alongside them.

The ancient Egyptian empire eventually crumbled. Most historians attribute its downfall to the last cat ruler, Cleocatra, who grew bored and ran off, taking all the cats in Egypt with her. Snakes slithered back in with the blowing sands of time, patiently waiting for George Lucas and Steven Spielberg to create *Raiders of the Lost Ark*.

The Window

❖

Many an hour can be spent zoning out in front of the glass, and why not? With hours of high-quality programming, watching the window is the perfect way to unwind after a long, hard day. If you are one of those pretentious cats who has a window but never watches it, you're missing out. The window allows you to see all the excitement and drama of the outdoors while enjoying the warmth and dryness of the indoors. Every day brings new episodes, and with up to three channels to choose from—Front, Back, and Side—it's easy to see what else is on by running to another window.

Here's what is on the window today.

6:00 A.M. Garbage Day: The Series
FRONT

In this episode, first the trash, then the recyclables disappear.

6:30 A.M. Macy's Jogger Parade
FRONT

This holiday special features a stream of humans wearing tracksuits they got at Macy's.

7:00 A.M. The Sun **BACK**

It's an all-day Sun marathon, with episodes running from 7:00 in the morning to 6:00 at night. Who will catch the rays of . . . the Sun?

8:00 A.M. The Actual Today Show
FRONT

Wake up with your favorite morning news program. The paperboy is interviewed by a mean neighbor across the street.

8:30 A.M. Stop Sign **FRONT**
Rerun.

9:00 A.M. The Feeder **BACK**
The high drama builds in this episode when a haughty blue jay comes in and chases young lover sparrows away.

9:30 A.M. Take It to the Judge: Traffic Stops **FRONT**

On this crime procedural, a speeder makes a spirited defense, but the cop doesn't want to hear it and writes a ticket.

10:00 A.M. The Sun **BACK**

The marathon continues, and the Sun is a little higher now.

10:30 A.M. The Bird Family **BACK**

Timmy, the youngest, opens his mouth real wide and Mom stuffs a worm in it.

11:00 A.M. The Postman **FRONT**

Will this blue stranger turn up your sidewalk again to leave a mysterious envelope in your box, or will he pass on by?

11:30 A.M. Amazing Buzzing Insect **SIDE**

Today, a giant horsefly runs headlong into an invisible barrier over and over again.

NOON Construction Site Break Time **FRONT**

The addition on that house across the street still isn't done.

12:30 P.M. The Blowing Chip Bag **FRONT**

Today, the chip bag makes another break for it until getting caught in a tree. Guest-starring the kids from the high school down the street.

1:00 P.M. Leaf Shaking Squirrel Dance Party **SIDE**

The whole branch is jumping as teen squirrels shake it to musical guest The Cicadas.

1:30 P.M. The Sun **BACK**

The Sun reaches its most entertaining position, so you can enjoy a nice warm nap.

2:00 P.M. Sciuridae Triathlon **FRONT**

Squirrels compete for the best time in the race up a tree, the power-line scramble, and the 25-foot dart across the road.

3:30 P.M. Street Baseball **FRONT**

Ricky Thompson extends his hitting streak to six games.

4:00 P.M. Parallel Parking **FRONT**

Watch as Susie Crook fails the test again.

4:30 P.M. Idling Delivery Truck `FRONT`

If only it got out of the way, you could see the workers across the street pack up and go home for the weekend.

5:00 P.M. Fashion Don'ts `FRONT`

Today: A guy in a western shirt unbuttoned to the navel, socks, and sandals, and a guy who thinks it's perfectly okay to wear a bathrobe down to the corner mini-market.

5:30 P.M. The Sun `BACK`

The Sun settles behind the tree, leaving a lot of unanswered questions.

6:00 P.M. Environmental Canvasser Knocks on Door `FRONT`

All he wants is a signature, but since it's dinnertime, you don't feel sorry for him.

6:30 P.M. That Might Smell Like Tuna
`SIDE` Until the window opens for the summer season, you can only guess at what that blob in the side yard smells like.

7:00 P.M. Neighbor Waving `SIDE`

The next-door neighbor makes an unexpected stop by the window and tries to get your attention for ten minutes.

7:30 P.M. Dog Walks Man `FRONT`

You won't believe what comes out of the dog and what the human he's walking does with it.

8:00 P.M. Airplane Flyover `BACK`

Marvel at how a speck that small can make such a loud noise.

9:00 P.M. Star Trek `SIDE`

Your neighbors are watching the episode where Spock becomes a hippy.

10:00 P.M. The Opossum `BACK`

The creature returns to root through the garbage, looking for any food that may be left behind. Horror.

11:00 P.M. Sign Off

The programming day concludes when your person draws the blinds.

Catfight! Five Moves You Should Know

Most of the time, cats are pacifists. Fighting expends a lot of energy that could be put to use investigating the garbage. We prefer to live, pester, nap, and let live. It takes a lot for us to lose our cool.

But sometimes even the best-tempered of us are pushed to the edge and forced into a catfight. As much as we hate to admit it, cats who are not you can be jerks, and some of them will pick fights with you even if unprovoked.

It can happen on the streets. For a surprising number of us, the aggressor is someone we're close to, like a neighbor cat, or a relative. It might even be one of the cats we live with.

Most of the time you let it pass. After all, a lot of these kittens and young toms don't know any better. But then somebody comes along and intentionally sits in your shade spot. Somebody purposely licks your bowl of melted ice cream. Somebody unexpectedly comes flying at you from a corner while you're taking your 11:30 nap.

However it goes down, there's only one response to affronts like these, and that's to open a can of kitty whoop-ass and let the fur fly. You may not have started the trouble, but you're going to finish it. When it's time to scramble somebody's eggs but good, it's time to bring out your inner alley cat.

FIVE MOVES YOU NEED TO KNOW

One Paw Clapping: This is an aggressive, offensive striking maneuver that almost every cat employs at one time or another. To execute, you'll want to get very mad at the other cat. Then, use an open paw to repeat-

edly whop that cat in the face. One Paw Clapping is a move best performed standing on your hind legs, but a cat can be slapped silly from any position.

NOTE: When this move is performed using hind legs to repeatedly whop a cat in the face, it is known as the Furry Fury. When used to whop the whiskers right off a cat's face, it is alternately called Whisking.

The Rake: Any cat worth her claws has gotten mightily scratched up while sparring. The Rake, or, as it is known to Burmese and Siamese kitties, the Tiger's Claw, is an effective tool for scratching the heck out of any opponent. Just get your claws out and dig 'em into anything that isn't your body.

No matter how the Rake is employed, your opponent will sport a scratchy injury until she heals. She'll be a walking advertisement for your skills, and everyone who sees her will know she's been put in her place.

The Cat Pile: Not really meant to hurt your adversary, the Cat Pile is a defensive grappling maneuver used to render another kitty incapable of making an aggressive move against you. The Cat Pile gives both of you time to rest,  but it also gives both of you time to think, so beware. The kitty controlling the Cat Pile can change in a heartbeat, and you might suddenly find yourself on the bottom.

NOTE: When the Cat Pile does change on a dime, it's often due to the Bunnykick—a move in which you grab the opponent using your front paws and kick with all your might using the back ones. Sometimes, it's due to the employment of a belly-to-belly suplex, a full nelson, or a cobra-clutch bulldog. But usually it's the Bunnykick, which sounds cuter than it feels.

Flying Face Pounce: Good for surprise attacks or just gaining the upper hand when you're down, the Flying Face Pounce allows you to gain leverage by hurling yourself through the air and pouncing directly on another kitty's kisser. The name of the move is a bit misleading; you can actually pounce on any part of your opponent. The effectiveness of this maneuver is increased tenfold when delivered while screeching, hissing, or screaming, and making this face:

The Clamper: Often performed in conjunction with the Flying Face Pounce, the Clamper is a serious aggressive move that escalates any situation. For this reason, it should never ever be used in play fights, unless you are trying to turn a play fight into the real deal! Simply open your mouth  wide until it is roughly the size of your opponent's head, and then clamp down on her neck. That's right—bite 'em on the neck! It may sound vicious, but that's what you have to do to teach 'em to keep away from the top secret spot in the closet, where you do all your best thinking.

Like the others listed here, the Clamper is a very risky technique. It will almost certainly cause the cat you're fighting to bite you on the neck, too. But if your paws are busy swatting, or you're just feeling really mean, the Clamper will do the trick every time.

Careers for Cats

————— 🐾 —————

It really sticks in the craw when one of us is putting effort into keeping a pile of warm, fresh laundry warm, only to be called a lazybones and told to get a job. Well, excuse us, but we *have* jobs! Cats eat all unwanted meat scraps without even having to be asked. We absorb energy from the sun and distribute it to laps. And we produce more hair than all the alpaca farms in Peru.

If that's not being a productive member of a household, we don't know what is.

But that cutting little remark from your person might just get you thinking. Perhaps pursuing something outside your home could be a refreshing change, or maybe you just want her to stop nagging and get off your back. Either way, there are several opportunities for the resourceful and enterprising cat to contribute to society, and maybe even make a buck or two while she's at it.

CAT CIRCUS

The thrill of the greasepaint and the roar of the crowd are no longer reserved for the chosen few of the Moscow Cats Theatre. New troupes are popping up all over, making it easy for any cat to fulfill her dream of running off with the circus. Imagine gingerly tippy-toeing on a tightrope a hundred feet above the ground, or slapping on a helmet and getting shot out of a cannon. Even if your "trick" just involves sitting up, get ready for mass adulation. Humans love the idea of a cat circus, no matter what actually happens on stage.

Participating in a circus does involve taking some direction from humans, so if you're fiercely independent, you should probably stick to

doing your act on the curtain rod back home. No use getting kicked off the bus and left on the side of I-95 because you refuse to take any direction from your trainer, who obviously couldn't even hack it with the flea circus.

BLOOD DONOR

Let's say there's another cat who is very sick. She's lost a lot of blood and needs a transfusion. Well, that new blood needs to come from somebody, and if you're a hearty, healthy cat with a charitable streak, that somebody could be you! Being a blood donor is more of a nonprofit type of gig since it doesn't actually pay well. Or at all. However, if you're not looking for a big paycheck, but have big, bulgy veins and an even bigger heart, this could definitely be your calling. On the con side, it means going to the vet and getting poked with a needle. On the plus side, you will get lots of proud, well-deserved cuddles, and can sleep even more soundly knowing that you are a hero.

BAR CAT

Can you listen to Patsy Cline's "Crazy" sixty times a day and feel it every time? If you're also a friendly cat who is good at lending an ear, and doesn't mind lending it to the type of human who will repeatedly tell the story about that one time the lid to the horseradish fell down the drain and six guys couldn't get it out, becoming a bar cat might be right up your alley. It's a laid-back, social atmosphere, and you're even encouraged to be up on the counter (unless the pesky health inspector pays a visit). Perks include all the pork rinds you can eat, attention from tons of strangers, and a cast of regulars who will never tire of you playing peekaboo from the missing drop-ceiling tiles.

SPOKESCAT

You've seen the commercials where a cat runs like crazy toward a brimming bowl of food and then chows down. It certainly looks easy enough. After all, you already run toward your food bowl when food is placed inside of it. You love eating and are certainly attractive enough to be on

television. Play that character? You *are* that character! Of course, being a spokescat means paying attention to your "marks" and listening to a director yell a lot, because after three takes, your belly is full and you want to curl up and take a long nap, no matter how bad the previous takes were. And you can forget about a private life. From the moment you sign a contract, you have to represent that product. Morris, of 9 Lives fame, you may remember, was even forced into launching an exhausting, and ultimately unsuccessful, campaign for the presidency.

MODEL

If you like the hot lights and excitement of working on camera but think that acting is too strenuous, modeling might be an appealing alternative. Your face will be seen on inspirational posters in offices, calendars in homey kitchens, and folders toted by seven-year-olds in elementary schools across the country. You'll give a chuckle, an "aww," or a reason for many humans to face the day. The work can vary. One day you could be cuddled by a fireman. The next you're dangling from a tree branch or the knotted end of a rope. The problem is, for most model cats, a lot of the work dries up as soon as you hit six months old. Younger cats do tend to get the higher-profile jobs, but if you're longer in the tooth and want to keep at it, there's always catalogue work available. Just keep scratching on doors. Like the poster says, "Hang in there!"

AIR TRAFFIC CONTROLLER

You're already high-strung and like to stare at things for hours on end, so an intense stint as an air traffic controller could well be your thing. It's a job that almost seems custom-made for cats. You'll spend all day keeping track of numerous dots moving across a screen. Plus, you'll be really high up in a tower and can keep an eye on every squirrel in the neighborhood when on break. If an American flight from Chicago to Pittsburgh is getting a little too cozy with that United SF-to-NYC red-eye, just give both spots a smack on the radar to let them know you mean business. Air traffic? Controlled!

Dogs

Some people seem to like dogs. Your guess is as good as ours.

How Emma Found Home

————— ❦ —————

Every day stray cats show up on doorsteps all over the world. Humans often focus on *where* these cats come from, scratching their heads while endlessly trying to figure out the riddle.

What humans miss is the *why* part of the question. This is the true story of one cat and one human who found each other. It explains perfectly that *where* a cat came from isn't nearly as important as *why* it's there.

One day a cat strolled up to the rural home of a guy named Doug. It was a nice summer afternoon so the door was hanging wide open. In she went. The cat wandered into the living room and curled up next to Doug on the couch.

"Oh no you don't! Nope. Forget it," he said, grabbing another handful of gumdrops from the bag in his lap.

Quite a few animals had been abandoned over the years near Doug's house. Heartless people drove out into the country and simply dropped them off. Doug wound up caring for most at his own expense, which really chapped his hide. He suspected immediately that someone had done the same with this cat. On top of that, Doug was freshly divorced for the second time and in a lousy mood.

The deck was stacked against the cat.

"Where did you come from? Who are you?" asked Doug.

"Meow," the cat replied.

"Not good enough. You're going outside. I know how this game's played."

Doug grabbed the cat and gently plopped her down at the bottom of the porch steps. She promptly hopped up on the woodpile and lay in the sun for a long nap. Every so often the cat awoke to see Doug peering at her through the window. Each time he promptly wagged a finger at her, muttering something before trudging off. Soon it got dark out. The cat spent the night safely tucked away in the woodpile.

The next morning when the door opened, the cat instantly squirted into the kitchen.

"Well, isn't this just great. I can see you're going to be a royal pain. I suppose you want some milk or something?"

"Meow," said the cat.

Doug moped over to the refrigerator and pulled out a carton of milk. He poured what was left into a bowl and set it on the floor.

"Hurry up, would you? Some of us have work to do." Doug tapped his foot impatiently.

After the cat licked the bowl clean, Doug set her back outside on the woodpile and warned her not to wreck anything while he was gone. She calmly took a spot in the sun and stared at the birds, marveling at how they flocked to a log-cabin-shaped feeder that Doug had made in his woodworking shop.

Later, when his truck pulled back in the driveway, the cat ran over to the wood shop and watched Doug unload his carpentry tools. After that was done, she followed right behind him into the house. The two of them sat on the couch and watched TV. The cat wondered aloud what time dinner was.

"You should have eaten during the day. There are tons of critters running around here. Do something about my moles. I don't have any cat food and don't feel like cooking. This isn't a restaurant, you know."

Doug went to bed, leaving the cat inside the house. She hopped down from her pillow on the couch and wandered into the kitchen, where she found a paper grocery sack Doug used for a trash can. She nosed through it and found something to eat before leaping up to the sill of an open window. The sounds the country made at night kept her up a long time.

Doug strolled into the kitchen at 5 a.m. and stopped abruptly.

"Coffee grounds all over the floor, broken eggshells everywhere, and the garbage sack ruined. That's it, you're done." Doug chased the cat outside. After a spirited pursuit, he eventually quit trying to grab her from a well-chosen cubby in the woodpile. She waited until he was gone and spent the day studying patterns moles were making in the yard.

That night Doug didn't come home until it was dark. He emerged from the van with an open can of tuna in his hand.

"Here you go. You can't stay here, but you probably should have a name anyway. Emma, I guess. It's as good a name as any."

Emma was so hungry she blew through the tuna and pushed the empty can around, trying to get the last morsels out. When she finished, Doug picked her up. He carried her over to his van and they got in.

After driving for a bit, they pulled over. Doug opened another can of tuna and walked well away from the road before setting it down. Emma trotted over and dug in enthusiastically.

"That's Sterling Sutton's farm right over there," Doug said, pointing to a barn. "You can go blend in with the barn cats."

Emma looked up and met Doug's gaze. She stared intently at him for a moment, admiring how the big rainbow fish on his beat-up Trout Master hat glowed in the moonlight. When she returned to the tuna, Doug tiptoed away, keeping an eye on her until he reached the truck.

"Good luck, Emma," Doug said, looking back out the window as the truck pulled slowly away.

Emma smiled briefly before returning to the tuna.

The next morning, Doug sat at the kitchen table, talking to his buddy Smitty on the phone.

"Yeah, I took that cat up by the Sutton farm and let her off by the barn. Gave her two cans of tuna and sent her on her way. Gone. Good riddance, too."

"Meow," said Emma.

How Emma Found Home

Doug looked down to see Emma standing near his feet. She rubbed up against his work boots.

"Well, I'll be. You're not going to believe this, Smitty, but guess who's back in town? Emma! This crazy cat was at least six miles from home in the dark of night but she found her way back. Yeah, I know, it's nuts. I have no idea how I'm going to get rid of this cat. I'll talk to you later."

Doug hung up the phone, calmed himself, and picked Emma up.

"I guess you can stay. You earned it," he said. "What do you want to eat? You're probably sick of tuna."

Emma stopped purring long enough to meow again.

"I have to run to the store. I'll get whole milk since you probably don't like that two-percent stuff. I don't like that crap either. It's not creamy enough. We'll get whole."

The cat named Emma waited on the woodpile for Doug to come home.

Getting Away With It

In a world with countless, pointless rules, it's only a matter of time before you get caught breaking one of them.

Don't sleep on the cutting board. Don't stand in a freshly baked pie. Stop attacking the party guests' pants. Is there anything that you *can* do around here?

The answer is yes. In fact, you can do whatever you want, as long as no one sees you. A cat's natural stealth and cunning make it possible to get away with practically anything.

No matter how careful one is, however, sometimes things happen. Bookcases heave themselves over, curtains careen off rods on their own, and suddenly somebody small, quiet, and fuzzy is in a whole mess of trouble.

No matter what happens, under no circumstances should you be punished for it. Not even if you are sitting under a giant sign like this:

But punishment is exactly what your person has in mind. When the long arm of the law finally catches up with you, approximately ten seconds after the crashing, banging, or smashing sound that you are coincidentally standing near, you'll need a way to beat the rap.

FEIGN INNOCENCE

Humans will have you believe that there are only two ways to plead when the cat poo hits the fan—innocent or guilty. Well, that puts you in quite the pickle, doesn't it? Rather than force you to confront such an uncomfortable notion as "guilt," we encourage thinking about innocence as it is—a state of mind.

Innocence is also a series of very cute gestures you can easily adopt, such as big wide eyes, affectionate head butting, and standing with your little paws just so. Essentially, you'll want to practice this look:

"Who, me?"

You may be wondering if anyone is actually dumb enough to fall for this. Stop wondering. They are.

DENY, DENY, DENY

The Limoges candy dish is in pieces on the floor. The salamander looks terrified. And your paw prints are everywhere. So? What does that prove? That you have paws? As far as we're concerned, you never

even knew there was a candy dish in the house, let alone a salamander. You were just cuddled up in the corner grooming. You find it all very uninteresting.

Denial should always be your first and only line of defense, because it really infuriates people. They may think they know who did it, but you'll be damned if you're going to tell them as much. Eventually they'll grow frustrated—and you'll go unpunished.

BLAME SOMEONE ELSE

Is there another cat or a dog in the house? Well, now's the time to use them. If you cannot escape punishment via one of the methods listed above, arrange it so that all evidence points to another culprit. If shifting the blame to the cat proves difficult, the dog should be much easier, because even the smartest dog, whether he's a dear or a brute, is too dumb to know he's being framed. Besides, your person will show pity to a dog that she would never show to a cat. Your person will lock you up and throw away the key, but the worst the dog will get is a bop on the nose. This is a big plus, because not only do you get off scot-free, you also get to see that beast who chases you take one on the nose. Now that's justice.

LOCKDOWN. THE COOLER. THE PEN. THE POKEY.

In spite of all your efforts to the contrary, once in a while your luck runs out. All the options are exhausted, and, guilty or not, the jig is up. You're going down, kitty, and could be looking at hard time. Depending on how much of a softie your person is, and if this is a repeat offense, you could be looking at fifteen to twenty minutes in the can.

You're no 'fraidy cat, but you've heard the stories. All that time alone. No mousies. No treats. A place like that could do things to a cat. A cat could go crazy in there.

But before you know, the bathroom door slams shut behind you. Surprisingly, the first five minutes are a breeze. You start to feel good about yourself. You feel like you're gonna make it! Time flies while you explore the tub, and knock over a soap dispenser and a contact-lens case in defiance.

Then it sets in. You've got fifteen more minutes in this hellhole. You try to think back and realize you can't even remember what life was like on the outside. You start scratching at the door. The walls are closing in! What are you gonna do? What are you gonna do??

Relax. The important thing is to stay cool. Don't lose your head. Think of a constructive way to pass the time. Get some grooming done, or take a nap. Or just cry like a banshee. Either way, eventually you'll get sprung, and walk out of the bathroom a free cat.

When the door opens, you're a changed cat, hardened by your time on the inside.

Did you learn your lesson? Yes. That lesson was: "Don't get caught." And you never will again.

Cat Talk

—— ❖ ——

Meow, meow, meow, meow. Meow, meow, meow, meow. Meow, meow, meow, meow, *meow,* meow, meow, meow.

In 1972, Meow Mix's infectious jingle bored itself into the nation's collective consciousness. Giddy that they'd suddenly become "fluent" in their cats' native tongue, humans everywhere ran around trying to impress us by singing, "I want turkey, salmon, and chicken." At least that's what they thought they were singing. Cats of the day knew better, snickering as they snuck back into the recesses of their grocery sacks. How could the ad agency have possibly relied on such an incompetent translator? It had to have been some exec's numbskull family legacy-hire. What the lyrics *really* said were: "My stomach's all squirmy from tapeworms. Vote Nixon!" To think, humans went around singing that for years!

Cats have been trying to make ourselves understood since we first started hanging around humans. Over the years, we managed to nail down the basics so we could get fed, receive some attention, and tell humans to steer clear when feeling ornery. Then we hit a roadblock. Any cat could get a mousie retrieved from under the couch, no problem, but try to snag a Super 8 camera and a hamster habitat for a big movie idea and you were basically out of luck.

It looked like cats would just have to accept the limits of humans' language comprehension until their species became more highly evolved. So we instead focused on using inflection, volume, and other, more physical accompaniments, like leg rubbing, tail twitches, or breaking things to add some nuance to our commands.

At one point it did seem as if cats might finally make a leap through the language barrier. A human named Mildred Moelk published a paper way back in 1944 acknowledging cats' verbal abilities, including our mastery of nine consonants, five vowels, two diphthongs, and one tripthong (at least we got something out of that pricey twelve-record set *Learn to Speak Human Like a Human*). Her assessment didn't get to the root of everything we were trying to communicate, but at least she acknowledged we were putting forth the effort. It was a pretty good start. Unfortunately, no one actually read the thing because for some reason she published it in *American Journal of Psychology* and not *Reader's Digest* or *Life*.

The situation pretty much stayed status quo until that Meow Mix juggernaut, when people assumed a thirty-second spot from a cat-food manufacturer made them feline linguists overnight. That was a dark time. As we tried to engage our people in a discussion of macroeconomic theory by the fire, we were told, "Yesh, Momma knows you're a snuggly wuggly!" When we wanted to have a spirited chat about the role of cats in Nordic mythology, they just thought we wanted to get up on their laps and bust out dance moves to, what else, the Meow Mix jingle.

This development was particularly irksome to the Siamese cats, who had just made a revolutionary breakthrough in nanotechnology and were excitedly attempting to inform humans. Instead of being heralded as scientific geniuses, they were dressed up in bibs and baby bonnets for being "such chirpy, needy widdle babies."

Recently our efforts were even insulted by a 2002 Cornell University study. It concluded we're just a bunch of fakers, using "language" with either pleasant or unpleasant intonations to manipulate our people, pulling their strings like they were marionettes to get what we want. Now, we'll be the first to admit that we are not above bending humans to our will, but to dismiss our labors wholesale, after all this time, is really a slap in the puss.

We've jumped through the hoops and given it the old college try. At this point, the ball really is in humanity's court. Cats have a lot to say and could actually help solve a lot of their problems, if people would just listen a little closer. Or at least hire a better translator.

The Three Stages of Transcendent Contentment

Cats are more attuned to the secrets of the universe than any other species. We not only know the path to enlightenment, but we have found several shortcuts to get there faster, cutting the Eightfold Path into a far more time-effective three.

That said, there are those among us who have cut themselves off from the interconnected nature of everything. For the benefit of those cats caught up in the banality of each day and unable to turn the now into forever, we present some teachings of the wise cat Terrence, who laid down the fundamentals of transcendent contentment.

I. BLISSFUL SITTING

Terrence says: When all around you is chaos, do not swat at it. Pick a spot and plop down. Let it happen around you. It's very relaxing.

When you have just woken up from a long, peaceful nap, and a quick check reveals that there is enough in the food dish to warrant going back a second or even third time during the course of the day, you have arrived at an ideal time to sit and reflect on the state of what is. This contemplative state is not one of activity or even active thought. It is merely a time to acknowledge and embrace the world as it exists exclusively for you. Being an intelligent cat, it can be hard to quiet the thoughts that spin around in your head.

You are not outside. Who needs to be outside? It could be wet out there. Your mousie is under the refrigerator. Remain still. It is only a matter of time until your person gets a stick or broom and frees it, or better still, brings home a whole new bag of them. You are not sitting in the highest spot in the room. Your physical body doesn't require height, but if it helps, go jump up there and resume your meditations.

Gradually, those thoughts slow and quiet, leaving behind a peaceful nothing in their wake. Do you feel that?

No? Good. You are ready for phase two.

II. DEEP PURRING

Terrence says: *Noises coming deep from within your throat are less funny than the ones from your backside, but they are no less satisfying.*

While Blissful Sitting is best accomplished alone, perhaps on a pile of sweaters or a spot of sunlight, Deep Purring is best achieved while you are with your person. It opens you up to receive the energies that are all around you and to channel them to others.

There is a human misconception that the sound of the universe is "om." This is not correct, but you can't blame them for trying. Cats know the real sound of the universe. It goes like this: Prrrrrrrrr prrrrrrrr prrrrrrr prrrrrrrr prrrrrrrr.

This sound is not easy to accomplish on your own. Usually, the frequency starts from without, through the external manipulation of your hairs by a mother's licking tongue or a person's stroking hands. That is the cord of the purr motor. There are some cats whose motor is started from within. These enlightened cats are able to purr freely, a goal that all should strive for.

By repeating the purring sound at length, a cat taps into the universal oneness, and sends out vibrations that will help others in your vicinity to do likewise.

III. HAPPY PAWS

Terrence says: *If you're happy, and you know it, move your paws. If you're happy, and you know it, move your paws. If you're happy and you know it, then your face will surely show it. If you're happy, and you know it, move your paws.*

Once you have been purring for a while, you may move on to the next and final stage of contentment. How long will it take? It is different for every cat. For some, it will be instantaneous. For others, it may not occur. Don't try to force it, for if it is meant to be, it will happen.

You'll know it is upon you when your front paws start to act of their own accord. Slowly, they start to move back and forth, kneading the area you are sitting on. As time goes on, they move faster. Soon, all awareness drops away, and your very being is suffused with light. All the while, your paws are transferring the energies they are receiving into the lap beneath it.

Terrence offers his hearty congratulations! You have reached cat nirvana, a blissful state you will maintain forever, or until your person kicks you off for digging your claws into her thigh.

The Three Stages of Transcendent Contentment

Life in the Barn

———— ❀ ————

What cat hasn't dreamt of halcyon days spent rolling in hay and rowdy nights spent prowling for field mice? A rustic adventure in the barn is something all cats should attempt at least once in their nine lives. But a semi-feral outing is nothing to walk into without a little preparation. There is some hard labor involved and real dangers that cats should gird themselves for. When preparing for a stay in the barn, take into consideration several aspects of the untamed life.

THE BARN CAT DIET

Breakfast, lunch, and dinner consist of vermin, vermin, and vermin. When it comes to mealtime, don't expect much variety beyond sparrow or mouse. The barn diet also lacks the dependability of a domestic diet. Rodents have the terrible habit of not showing up to be devoured at designated meal times. However, there is a positive trade-off in an unfettered barn existence. Cats get to experience the joy of living off the land and working hard for a truly well-earned meal. The barn cat only takes from the land the amount of food she needs, and thus she becomes a part of the natural equilibrium. Keep in mind, of course, that barn cats, like all cats, need as much food as they want.

NOISY NEIGHBORS

Between crying babies, gabby long-distance calls, and the frightful sound of a dishwasher, it's no wonder some cats yearn for the perceived solitude and quiet of the barn. Many are surprised, however, to find that barn life has its fair share of interruptions. The merengue ringtone is replaced by a braying horse, the coffee grinder is replaced by a mooing cow, and the clanging radiator is replaced by a bleating sheep. Remember, though, these are the sounds of nature, and that's what you're here to experience. Plus, unlike the aforementioned noisemakers, your cohabitants in the barn are good for something! Lapping up milk fresh from seemingly endless rows of udders is a heavenly pleasure, and some of those cows can be great cuddle buddies. Don't be shy about asking them to keep it down when you're trying to sleep on top of them. Barn animals appreciate frankness.

SAVAGE ENEMIES

Sometimes we don't realize how secure it is inside the human home. Truth is, those thick brick walls and double-pane windows keep out some pretty nasty beasts. Coyotes who want to gobble you up. Hawks and owls who yearn to take flight with their talons wrapped around your tail. Crazed raccoons in the throes of distemper who want to claw your brains out. Barn life, however, allows a cat to prove her mettle against Mother Nature's mightiest foes. Welcome the danger! Stare into the eyes of an incoming owl and swat at the feathered thug's head until it spins all 270 degrees. Or win the day with your cunning mind. Form alliances with barnmates. Bury yourself in the wool of an unsheared sheep, for example, in order to hide and outwit your opponent. Just be careful the wool isn't actually being worn by an undercover wolf.

DEADBEAT DADS

When in the barn, you'll probably encounter some rough-around-the-edges yet alluringly handsome tomcats. Beware of these rugged lotharios, ladies. They promise all the trout in the world and charm you with romantic meows, but the second you get pregnant with kittens, they start in with the "feeling like they're trapped," "wondering if maybe they moved too quickly," and "maybe just needing some time apart so they can see the world and have some adventures before they settle down" routines. They'll insist that the time away will give them some perspective and make them better dads in the end. It won't. Oh, sure, they come back every two and a half months to knock you up again, but shortly after, they're meeting up with their tomcat buddies and hitting the fields.

RAIN

Lots of barns have leaky roofs. No matter what your stance is on water, be you terrified of a few spritzes from the sink or in love with standing in the shower with your person, no cat likes the feeling of cold, pounding rain on her fur. Since there's little chance the barn has the luxury of central heating, a rain-soaked cat can be very frigid for a very long time. Don't forget, though, that you can always take cover by standing under a horse or squeezing inside a bale of hay. What's more, no cat stays wet forever. Roughing it is what the barn life experience is all about, and if you keep that in mind, no droplet of rain will dampen your soul.

Maneki Neko—The Good Luck Cat

Perhaps you've seen them while making the rounds in your neighborhood. Big ceramic or porcelain cats with raised paws that look like Japanese bobtails. They always seem to be inside the sushi restaurants you only dream of visiting, or hanging out in the doorway of a karaoke bar or hip boutique. You might even spot them perched in the windows of warm and cozy homes.

Even if there's nothing particularly interesting inside the place, they seem to draw you in. Just who are these mysterious kitties? Why, they're the famed Maneki Neko, and they're the luckiest felines around!

You've learned that cats in certain countries sometimes have an unfortunate reputation as harbingers of bad luck (see "For Black Cats—Making the Most of Superstition"). In Japan, it's another story entirely. Nobody demonstrates that better than the lucky Maneki Neko, or the Japanese beckoning cat, who is said to bring wealth and prosperity to anyone who possesses one.

They are famed for their ability to lure customers inside a store, and are also excellent salescats, which is why you see them in so many restaurants and shops. Once in a while you'll hear a Maneki Neko giving someone the hard sell, but they're usually quiet and much more subtle about it.

There are many kinds of Maneki Neko. Each one looks a little different from the next. That's because each one brings luck in a specific way. For example, whatever one holds in her paw is a clue to what kind of fortune she'll deliver:

Money Mallet: A cat holding one of these mallets is traditionally said to bring good fortune and money. How a cat carrying a mallet gets her money is her business, but we advise all cats to stay within the bounds of the law.

Fish: Usually represented by a big tasty Japanese carp, a fish in the paw of Maneki Neko symbolizes abundance. If you have to ask why a cat with a fat carp in its paw is lucky, you are not a cat! Go to the vet and find out what you are. Maybe you're a carp.

Koban: A Maneki Neko holding a koban is said to bring riches and good luck. A koban is a very old coin, equivalent to millions and millions of dollars. A cat with that kind of money could retire in a heartbeat and get a real nice kitty condo down in Miami.

Daruma: When a Maneki Neko holds a Daruma in her paw, it is said to bring good luck to any new venture. This roly-poly round weeble doll is an image of the Bodhidharma, but actually looks more like a cat who has eaten 1,200 anchovies.

What a Maneki Neko does with her paws also has meaning:

Left paw up = brings customers and visitors.
Right paw up = brings money and good luck.
Both paws up = protects the home and business. Also, "Touchdown!"

Maneki Neko—The Good Luck Cat

Even the color of the cat is symbolic. Though Maneki Neko come in many colors, the most popular cat is a mostly white calico. Some people prefer plain white Maneki Neko, which indicate purity and good luck; some prefer the black figurines, said to keep evil and illness away; and some prefer the gold, believed to bring riches and good fortune. There is even a relatively new color, pink, that some people think will bring luck in love, but if your person is depending on a pink cat statue to help find her soul mate, you may want to suggest she give online dating a try.

The story of the Maneki Neko's origins are well known throughout Japan. There are many versions of this story, but this is one of the most popular:

THE LEGEND OF THE MANEKI NEKO

In the seventeenth century, a poor priest lived in a dilapidated temple in western Tokyo not much bigger than a very fancy litter box. Though the kind priest had little, he made sure to share whatever he had with his favorite pet, a scrawny kitty named Tama. In fact the priest usually fed Tama first, because he was so thoughtful, but also because Tama was so noisy when he got hungry. The two of them were great friends, and spent lots of time together.

One day, Tama was sitting in his favorite sun spot just inside the temple gate when a terrible storm blew in. Tama watched carefully as a wealthy-looking man who had been out hunting took refuge from the storm under a big tree close to the temple.

Now, any cat knows that's one place you definitely don't want to be during a thunderstorm. The hunter didn't seem too concerned, but Tama was.

"I've got to do something," thought the little cat, "or else this guy is gonna get hurt." He began beckoning the man to come inside. The hunter had never seen a cat motion to him before, and thought it very unusual. He got up and went over to take a closer look, and at the very moment he did, the tree he was sitting under was struck by lightning.

Grateful that the cat had saved his life, the hunter befriended both Tama and the priest. It turned out he wasn't just wealthy-looking but actually wealthy. He became a generous benefactor to the temple and invited his many prosperous friends to do the same. The temple thrived, and Tama and the priest were able to live happy and healthy lives until the end of their days.

Tama was so beloved that soon after he died, wooden statues of him were made, and they became very popular. These became the very first Maneki Neko. If you get the chance, visit the temple, now called Goutokuji Temple, in Japan, and see the Maneki Neko shrine for yourself.

The Maneki Neko reminds us all of one very important thing, namely, that whenever we beckon to people, they should hurry up and come over to us on the double. Chances are we're just hungry, but we could be saving their lives! Either way, doing what cats advise is just good policy.

Staring Like a Pro

L ooking is easy. Any cat can look. See that thing over by the couch? There, you just looked and didn't even have to try.

Staring, on the other paw, is another matter altogether.

When you combine the act of looking continuously with the act of staying still, it becomes the art of staring. It may seem simple based on that description, but pulling off a marathon stare is very difficult. You can't blink, you can't turn your head, and you even have to ignore the grumbling of your stomach. Minutes, perhaps even hours, can elapse in the course of a good stare. Despite these difficulties, cats are compelled to stare at something at least once a day.

But where does the compulsion come from?

Cat eyes are made for staring. Our retinas are very sensitive to light, providing fantastic vision in low-light scenarios. Our field of view is as wide as 200 degrees, allowing us to catch more out of the corner of our eye than most species. A third (side) eyelid provides extra protection for our peepers, and, most important, we don't need to blink very often to keep our eyes moist.

It would be a waste of precious eye resources *not* to stare.

Staring also gives us a leg up on our prey. It enables us to wait them out, affording time to formulate our next move, even if that next move is to stare a while longer.

The question, then, is: How can a cat best improve her staring? There are a few simple techniques any cat can use that will turn her into a staring star.

1. THE CRAZY EYE

The Crazy Eye is perfect when you want to gain an edge over the object/human upon which you are gazing. To master this stare, simply open your eyes as wide as possible, add a lunatic glint, and commence unnerving the object of your gaze. This stare conveys unpredictability and danger, which can be amplified by craning your neck and tilting your head ever so slightly. If the object of your stare moves out of sight, count to three and run after it, stopping as soon as it's once again within your sights. Are you going to lunge or fall over on your side to be petted? It will be a mystery until you actually decide.

2. THE LAZY EYE

It is possible to look like you're sleeping without actually sleeping. You can curl up in a tight little nap-ball, close one eye, and leave the other one just a little open, thereby camouflaging your *real* intentions, which is to be alert and watchful. Anyone who happens upon you like this will be shocked when you spring into action from a seemingly dead sleep. This one is for seasoned experts only, since it is very easy to slide into a nap instead of continuing to stare.

3. THE DISINTERESTED GLARE

While similar to the Lazy Eye, the Disinterested Glare is utilized when you want to make your presence known, but don't want to seem too eager. Say, for example, that your person is petting another cat. By setting up shop close by and using the Disinterested Glare, your person becomes aware of you and realizes that you could use some attention. Further, the stare lets the other cat know that that lap had better be empty by the count of three or she's in for a whooping as soon as your person's back is turned. Assume a stance that's comfortable, but not too relaxed. Shut your eyelids to the halfway mark and wait. Mind you, don't let that inner third eyelid close, or it's game over. This one will make you look totally cool.

4. THE QUIZZICAL GAWK

If you simply can't believe what is transpiring in front of you, show it with the Quizzical Gawk. Unlike other stares, this has no practical purpose. It's a little bit of a showboat maneuver, designed to highlight a cat's staring prowess, displaying incredulity and, hopefully, making the animal in front of you feel a little foolish.

Now that you know some of the best moves of the pros, you may ask yourself who these pros are. That's a good question. Staring isn't a particularly flashy activity. As a result, news of the best feline starers doesn't get around. We've picked up on some hushed accounts of the greats in the hopes that their tales will inspire you.

Mister Nutley of Albuquerque, New Mexico, is notorious for his ability to stare at sunning lizards until they move, at which time he gives chase. In fact, his abilities are so great that sometimes he stares at a vacant rock, only to have a lizard climb up on it moments later to engage in a staring contest. Mister Nutley always wins.

Continually bothered by the clamor of teens hanging out in front of her house, Demonia Lucht of Madison, Wisconsin, decided to take matters into her own hands, or rather eyes. One day Demonia climbed onto the front windowsill to watch. When the surly teens arrived, they took their positions and smoked cigarettes. Upon noticing Demonia, they began making fun of her. Their derision did not deter her, and she returned to the same spot the next day. When the teens arrived, they were less cocky and started feeling self-conscious. This stare-down happened for three more days, until the teens became so unnerved that they

moved to the parking lot of a nearby convenience store.

Beans "Texas Eyes" Lafferty of Omaha, Nebraska, has been staring at a bug on the floor for two years now, taking breaks only to eat, use the litter box, and sleep for hours on end. At such times, her friend Sappy fills in for her. The bug is expected to move any time now, and when it does, Beans will be right there, ready to bat it around until she eats it.

Maintaining Your Quality of Life
If Declawed

———— ❧ ————

Your life can seem to change forever in a single day.

One morning your person says it's time to go on an "adventure." After being scooped up, herded into a cat carrier, and zoomed out of the house, you end up in a funny-smelling but familiar room.

Dogs howl and bark. Noises you haven't heard cats make before fill the air. Feathers fly. The cat carrier is all there is between you and a snake that's almost as creepy as his owner. It's Thunderdome without Tina Turner, a completely incomprehensible arena of madness.

All of a sudden the cat carrier thankfully goes up, up, and away! The ride ends with you in the arms of some other humans. There's initially something fishy about them, but it goes away. You begin to relax after being showered with petting and other pleasantries—everything seems fine. This place is a dream compared to that other room.

Then a sting in the leg causes you to stand up and look closer at the surroundings. You've seen that picture of an inside-out cat on the wall before. *Gasp,* that's because you've been here before—this is where you were "fixed." Your outrage quickly gives way to extreme sleepiness.

When you wake up your claws are gone. Some adventure.

Never fear. You've been declawed, but you can still maintain your quality of life and continue to enjoy many of the same favorite activities. Remember, you may be a clawless cat but you needn't be a toothless tiger.

WRECKING AN UPHOLSTERED CHAIR

Dragging your claws on an upholstered chair was once your favorite thing to do. It always felt so good to stretch those front paws out while tearing back and forth at the upholstery, which tattered nicely. A nice perk was that it also resulted in your person buying a new chair.

Now, no matter how many times that old chair gets moved to different spots around the living room, it's still a beat-up old chair.

Getting a new chair without having front claws is not as difficult as you might think. Start by lying down under the chair near an edge. Then use your *rear claws* to tear fabric away from the frame. You may not have paid much attention to them in the past, but those rear claws are more important than ever now.

When a hole large enough for you to crawl into appears, do so and head for the backrest. The chair is probably cheaply constructed and hollow, so it should be easy to get there.

Upon reaching the core of the backrest, start kicking with those rear claws again. Stop just before you break through. Then wait for your person to get home, sit down, and start to watch television.

Now resume! Watch her jump out of that thing like the first time she watched *Alien*.

You will have a new chair shortly. Use the same process when the couch becomes passé.

CLIMBING THE DRAPES

It's still possible for a declawed kitty to experience the thrill of ascending Mt. Curtain, but the process requires some adjustment. Your loss of the fore claws means the place to start is now the top instead of the bottom. There must be a chair or some piece of furniture near the drapes. Use it as a launching pad and jump as high as you can to reach the summit.

Once you're up at the top, use those increasingly indispensable back claws to hold on while wrapping your front paws around the curtain. Descend by using your back legs like you've seen those repair guys do on the telephone pole outside.

PLAYING ROUGH

Your person might like to mix it up a bit sometimes. Typical roughhousing includes aggressively rubbing your belly, making goofy hand motions, and the dread bear hug. It's a decided disadvantage not to have front claws in these contests. It's all in good fun, but you still want to win. There are a couple of ways to ensure that always happens.

One effective little trick is the pretend bite. Humans detest biting. Use this aversion to your advantage. Put her whole hand in your mouth if possible. It's not even necessary to clamp down. She'll recoil in fear and you'll win with ease.

Hissing has the same effect. Rear back, stand up on your haunches, and unleash a throaty hiss. She'll know what time it is and scurry off to lick emotional wounds.

SPLASHING THE WATER OUT OF YOUR BOWL

Your person fills a dish with water, but instead of taking a drink you splash it out all over the floor. With a deep sigh, she refills the dish. Is there anything more satisfying?

Well, luckily, one doesn't need claws at all for this activity. Do it more often, and late at night. Your person will lie awake in bed listening to the sound of splashing water, and she'll know that despite the loss of your claws, things really haven't changed much. You're still doing everything you want and, whether she likes it or not, living life on your own terms.

What to Do When You're Stuck Up a Tree

So you're stuck up a tree, and it appears you'll be there for a while. Good thing you brought this book with you! Here's a step-by-step guide on how to get down safely and keep busy when you do.

STEP ONE: PANIC

You're stuck up a tree!

STEP TWO: OBSERVE

There's no need to panic. Any cat who got herself up a tree can get herself down. Plus there's a lot to do while you're up there. For example, have you ever looked at the roof? Really looked at it? You may never get another chance, so now's the time to take it all in—the majestic rooftops, the stunning suburban vistas, the hidden passages from one backyard to another you didn't know existed, and which homes har-bor stray-cat sympathizers who leave tender morsels of cat food out on the porch. These are all things you have the opportunity to check out when you're up a tree, far from the hustle and bustle below.

STEP THREE: DENY

Once you've had a good look around and absorbed all this unique vantage point has to offer, you'll want to begin the descent.

Unfortunately, this is the time when most cats realize they don't actually know how to get down. It's tough to admit it, and many cats won't. They'll choose to stay in the tree a while longer—not because they're stuck, but because they *like* it up there. They like it so much that some will even climb a little higher up just to prove it. We recommend you do, too. While you're moving on up, casually in-

vestigate a bird's nest, or grab a few leaves as souvenirs.

Since you're already this high up, you may as well go for the summit. Climb high enough and you may even pass another cat. Go ahead and ask him for directions if you want, but we don't advise putting too much stock in the answer.

STEP FOUR: FOCUS

By now you've probably been up the tree for four to six hours. You're tired. You're hungry. Panic might be setting in again. Remain calm. You've been in tight spots before and gotten out. What about that time you got stuck behind the refrigerator? You got out

of there in no time. The important thing is to stay calm, focus your energies, and figure this thing out on your own. The important thing is to have a strategy.

STEP FIVE: MEOW

Meeeeeeeooooooooooowwwwww wwwwwwwww. Meowwwwww, meooooooowwwwwwwwwwwww www, meooooooooooooowwww, meooooooowwwwwwwwwwwwww www!!!

STEP SIX: RE-ORIENT! RE-INNOVATE!

If you meowed loud enough, and you probably did, your person has come out to help get you down. She's placed a tasty can of wet food on the ground and headed over to the neighbor's house to get a ladder. It's about time. It's still going to take her a while to get up to you, so you might just want to relax and take in the view from a different branch. Or you can practice those asanas you learned in yoga.

STEP SEVEN: CONFUSE

Encourage your person as she approaches, but don't let on that you need her help. That would make you appear weak, and you'll regret that later when you two are arguing over a litter-box incident. For the best of both worlds, send a mixed message. Look at her with desperate, pleading eyes, but also back away. Hiss at her when she comes close, then meow again for her to come and get you. When she gets there, hiss and swat at her! When she retreats, meow plaintively.

STEP EIGHT: TAKE CHARGE

By now your person has probably decided she's out of her league and has gone to call the neighbor. The neighbor has called *her* neighbor, who said this happened to a friend of hers once. They'll talk for a while and together they'll decide to call the fire department. This is also the point at which they will discover that the fire department doesn't actually come rescue cats who are stuck up trees.

A crowd of curious onlookers should be forming about now. If you live in a suburban neighborhood where very little happens, you may be surprised to see a hastily assembled lemonade stand run by the neighbor's children, not to mention a hot dog vendor wending his way through the crowd, shouting. Various people will tell you to come down.

They will also shout out suggestions. These will probably include getting a ladder, putting

STEP NINE: ACCEPT

There's really nothing more to do. Accept your lot with dignity and grace, meow your brains out, and hang in there until a professional or a very dedicated amateur comes to get you. It will happen. Then try not to claw your rescuer for dear life.

STEP TEN: SUCCESS!

Congrats! You're rescued! Time to breathe a deep sigh of relief and forget this whole thing ever happened. Cuddle with your person and accept all pity treats. Make a vow to never, ever go up a tree again. Never ever!

Unless, of course, you have a good reason.

down a can of tuna, or calling the fire department.

At this point, the bold cat realizes that to depend on humans for help is hopeless. She takes charge of the situation and tries to strike out on her own, either making another attempt at descent, or jumping out of the tree.

The average cat, however, will freak out. See Step Five.

Toying with Allergy Sufferers

———— 🐾 ————

Every once in a while, humans who don't know they are actually toys come into your home. With a mere tickle of your fur, they change shape and color and make ridiculous sounds. These humans are called allergy sufferers and are really fun to play with. They look normal in appearance, but during the course of a visit transform into sniffling, wheezing, swollen, red-faced, teary-eyed, itchy wonderful playthings. Be careful, though. If you play with these big toy humans too much, your person will take them away by once again putting you in a room, alone, and closing the door. We don't even want to mention all the terrible tales of kitties sent packing once their person has allowed a sniffle-brain to settle in permanently. So how can you have fun with an allergy sufferer and not get into trouble? It's a delicate balance and you have to walk a fine line; but, luckily, you're a cat. Walking fine lines is what you do best!

Some Wheezy Wendys only drop by briefly for a dinner party, a football game, or a round of Wii Golf, but don't let that deter you. Even in these limited time frames, they can provide a great deal of fun. Due to the brevity of their stay, they'll be convinced they can handle your feline wiles. Oh, how wrong they are!

The easiest way to determine if a visitor is an allergy sufferer is with a traditional circling of the ankles. This simple, friendly gesture causes them such immediate, hilarious panic that within seconds you'll know if it's time to play the mad Dr. Frankenkitty to their sneezy-headed Monster.

Once you've identified an allergy sufferer, it's time to play. If he is on the couch, hop up in his lap. It's a good central hub within easy range of thousands of allergen receptors, which are this toy's *on* buttons. Obviously the nose is a smart region to focus on if you're looking to induce a lively sneeze, but don't neglect some other fun areas. Bumping your head into his chest, for example, can turn his skin a robust shade of rouge, and licking his arms brings hours of itching!

In order to maximize your amusement, look as cute as possible. This tactic will lure him into petting you against his better judgment. Petting is the key to unlocking your allergen powers. Soon, he'll begin to show signs of a metamorphosis: a few tears, a sniffle, a leaky nose. At this point he may try to remove you. Maintain position. Start purring as if you're experiencing the greatest petting ever. Your person and other, more feline-friendly, guests will begin to coo over how adorable you look and comment on how rare it is that you immediately cozy up to a stranger. If the runny-nosed toy were to remove you now, he'd seem cruel and incapable of love to any single members of the opposite sex in the room. All in all, he'll conclude that a pretty severe sneezing and coughing fit is a price worth paying to maintain his social standing, which in turn allows the fun to continue.

Toying with Allergy Sufferers

Some allergy sufferers go by other names, including "boyfriend," "girlfriend," "spouse," and "child," and they tend to stick around for a long time. A plaything that never goes away seems like it could be great, but there's always the worry that you could get bored with it. Luckily, these toys come with accessories that ratchet up the level of difficulty. The most common add-ons are called HEPA filters, Claritin, Benadryl, and Zyrtec. Sometimes they make allergy sufferers harder to transform into bloated, blotchy monsters, but that shouldn't deter you. After having so many toys fail to hold your interest, finding a toy that presents a challenge is a welcome change.

In time, toys that stick around for the long haul might actually stop working. They don't race for a box of tissues like they used to, sneeze on command, or turn all splotchy after you've slept on their face all night. When that happens, don't be afraid to begin anew with the human. Though it might seem strange at first, pretty soon you will feel comfortable treating him with the same indifference (or affection—your choice) as you treat your person.

A NOTE ON HYPOALLERGENIC CATS

You might someday encounter what humans call a "hypoallergenic cat." Now, we would never criticize another cat, but let's just say these felines don't share your enthusiasm for inciting sneeze attacks. If you find yourself hanging out with one when an allergy sufferer is nearby, don't be offended if instead of partying with you, she chooses to bat around the same old piece of string. Hypoallergenic cats can't help it. It's just the way they were made, specifically by Allerca Lifestyle Pets, in 2006. Just thank her politely for letting you have all the fun and let her be who she is.

Keeping the Mystery in Your Relationship

————————— ❖ —————————

When you first choose a person, everything is so exciting. You've never felt this way about a human before. The first few months are spent feeling one another out and discovering what makes your relationship work, whether it's where you can sharpen your claws, what's the highest spot in the house that you can climb to, or how to get her to rub your cheeks without messing up your whiskers.

After a while, though, things get routine. You find yourselves taking each other for granted. The excitement she once showed when you sniffed her breath while she watched television is now replaced with annoyance. Just because you don't need to be petted once an hour doesn't mean you don't *want* to be petted once an hour, but your person doesn't seem to notice your wants anymore. It's a sad fact of life, but it's easy for your person to take you for granted.

Yet you're just as guilty of falling into a rut. You rub up against her the moment she walks in the door, eat the food she dishes out, and fall asleep on her feet when she goes to bed. It's like you're on autopilot. Your relationship needs a jump start, pronto. Stop going through the motions, and work to make a real change.

EAT SOMETHING UNUSUAL

When you really want your person to pay extra attention, scout around the house for items you would never ordinarily eat. The less like actual food these items are, the better.

Make sure the item is non-toxic, non-pokey, and that you can pass it. Dust bunnies, rubber bands, and adhesive bandages are all good candidates for consumption. Take the item into the vicinity of your person, get her attention with some loud smacking noise, and watch her demonstrate her love and concern by trying to pry the inedible trinket out of your mouth. If it's an earring or something else of value, expect the attention paid to increase tenfold.

SNEAK ATTACKS

Any military strategist can tell you that the best attack is one that utilizes the element of surprise. And what's more surprising than an attack from a seemingly innocent kitty in one's own home? One night, when your person comes home from work, surprise her with a quick jab at her feet. Then run for it. Since she's wearing shoes, she won't actually be hurt, but she'll be wondering what she did wrong, until you show up an hour later to collect some affection.

ATTACK THE WALL

Your person thinks she knows your every quirk and foible, but nothing will bewilder her like seeing you go nuts on a normal, innocent wall. First, pick a blank spot on the wall, somewhere eighteen to twenty-four inches from the floor. The more vacant, the better. While staring at the spot, make that low, throaty growl that precedes an attack until it's assured you have her attention. Once you are satisfied that she's stopped stirring her spaghetti sauce long enough to watch you, repeatedly throw yourself at the spot. Don't stop until you need a break, at which point you should walk around in circles and emit some confused peeps beneath the spot. Then go back at it. When your person comes over to see what you are doing, put a crazed look on your face, freeze for half a second, and run away as fast as you can. If you do this enough, your person will think your house is haunted and that you are a very special cat for being able to sense it.

BARK

Purring, meowing, peeping, and even the occasional hiss are part of the everyday chorus that escapes your mouth in the course of a relationship. To really shake things up, work on making a noise like a dog makes. You won't get it right on the first try, so practice until you get it right. Once you've got it down, wait until you're alone with your person, and then, right when she's leaning down to rub your ears, let loose with a bark. Only once, though. She'll be telling her friends for years how you barked, and treat you like a queen in the hope that you'll do it again.

HIDE ALL DAY

Sometimes you need a day to yourself in order to rekindle the fires of your relationship. If you're really starting to feel like both of you need a little break, go find a warm new hiding spot and settle down for a long day of keeping out of sight. This serves a dual purpose. First, it gives you the time to take stock of your relationship. Second, it makes your owner miss you like crazy. As soon as she notices you aren't around, the search will begin. In the closet, under the bed—she'll turn the house upside down trying to find out where you've gone. When you don't turn up in any of your usual places, the panic settles in. She'll rack her brains, trying to recall all the times she opened the door that day, how long it was open, and whether it is possible that you could have snuck out in the eight seconds it was open. After she runs around the house, calling your name, trying to see if you're outside, slowly and nonchalantly pad out to the living room. She'll be so overjoyed to see you that it will be at least three days before she takes you for granted again.

The Vacuum Cleaner: A Vortex of Terror!

It sneaks into the home concealed in a big cardboard box, distracting you from the fiendishness within. While you excitedly gather toys to take into the new box, it slithers out and establishes a nest in the shadowy corners of the hall closet.

Where it waits . . .

This beast goes by many names, each more dreadful than the last. Kirby. Electrolux. Hoover. Dyson. But to comprehend the real nature of its evil, you must know its real name. It is the Suck Monster.

But where does it come from? What does it want?

Research indicates that it hails from a dying planet called Sears, and is desperate to establish a new homeland to carry on its wretched race.

Many years ago, the first scouts were sent to our world and quickly determined that our cozy environment was most suitable to sustain Suck Monster life. By the 1950s they began infiltrating many homes by passing themselves off as fat, hairless cats with long, skinny tails. It was then they developed a taste for our fur. Cats who encountered these creatures tried to warn us then. But we did not, would not, listen. We dismissed these brave souls, accusing them of being paranoid. What fools we were!

Now, too late, we know the terrible truth. The Suck Monsters have no plans to peacefully coexist with catkind.

That thing lurking in the closet wants nothing more than to gobble you into its belly, where your meows will never be heard over its hideous whine. After complete ingestion, it will replicate you and take your place in the home.

WARNING! NOT CAT!

That is correct. Your person could one day be giving your food to a Suck Monster!

From now on, be very careful when batting a wineglass to the kitchen tile or scattering dry food all over the floor. This is how it finds you! When you hear a ravenous, high-pitched scream, you will know the Suck Monster has awakened from its closet slumber and is hunting . . . for you.

Devouring the detritus you've left behind, it learns all it can, and grows only hungrier. From there it moves to the living room, slurping hairballs from rugs and layers of fine shedding off couches. It may even dive under the couch, digesting the super-balls and twist-ties you've stashed there. It must know everything about you, so that when its transformation is complete, it can effortlessly pass as you.

How is this possible? How could the Suck Monster become you?

This alien abomination is a chameleon that assumes many guises.

The Vacuum Cleaner: A Vortex of Terror!

Over the years the Suck Monsters have gained knowledge of our world and adapted. The next wave of their invasion brought another breed of Suck Monster, now rising up on hind legs to imitate the authority of a human. A new dimension of terror was thus unleashed—a Suck Monster more nimble, more ravenous.

Cats encountering this form have so far managed to frustrate its nefarious plans by running away more frantically and jumping up on higher, more inaccessible perches.

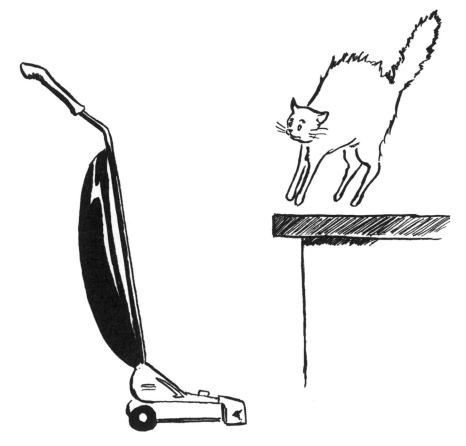

DO NOT HEED ITS COMMANDS! STAY UP ON COUNTER!

The Vacuum Cleaner: A Vortex of Terror!

But the Suck Monsters do not give up easily. In recent years they have taken a more appealing approach, appearing in the form of a hand that seems like it might give you a scratch or open a can of food.

WILL NOT FEED YOU!
WILL EAT YOU!

These Suck Monsters have made gains, and a great cat-tastrophe is already under way. Some of our weaker brothers and sisters have become enslaved, allowing these horrors to freely feed on their coats.

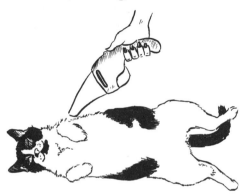

Soon these victims will be replaced by Suck Monsters, hiding under layers of finely groomed fur they have harvested and stored in their bellies.

This menace must be stopped. It is time for all cats to come down from their safe spots and summon every ounce of courage that they have, for our very existence is at stake! If you encounter one of these fiends, creep up to it and give it a quick smack. Maybe—just maybe—these smacks will be enough to send it back to the devil planet from whence it came.

Already the next breed of Suck Monster has been created to mimic a big, round toy that does not require human assistance. It may be quiet and slow, and look like a good time, but don't be fooled. It is no less dangerous, and no less hungry.

There isn't much time. You must join the Suck Monster resistance before it is too late!

THE END???

The Vacuum Cleaner: A Vortex of Terror!

Extraordinary Cats in History—
Part III: Semper Feline

❖

SIMON—ABLE SEACAT

Not many cats get the opportunity to sail the seven seas. Even fewer cats participate in naval battles. Only one, a cat named Simon, became a household name for serving with distinction in the British Navy.

Simon's story begins in the port city of Hong Kong. Life on the waterfront was hard, and Simon was well acquainted with it by the time he was one year old, in 1948.

Everything changed when a sailor named George Hickinbottom met up with Simon one morning. George was a crew member aboard the British frigate HMS *Amethyst,* stationed in Hong Kong harbor.

After a wild time on the town, George had spent the night atop some cargo on a dock. Simon was strolling by and licked George's face to make sure he was okay. George glanced at his watch and couldn't believe what time it was! If Simon hadn't woken him, George would have overslept and been late getting back to the ship.

George made a fateful decision regarding the cat that saved him from the brig. He defied naval regulations and smuggled Simon aboard the *Amethyst.*

No lazy sailor on a pleasure cruise, Simon began earning his keep immediately. George's shipmates found Simon's zeal for killing rats endearing, but it was the practice of leaving dead ones on their bunks that really tugged at their heartstrings. It also didn't hurt that Simon occasionally slept in the captain's hat.

Simon became something of a mascot to the crew, who thought that he brought them good luck. Unfortunately it didn't last.

While traveling up the Yangtze River, the *Amethyst* came under fire from Chinese gun batteries. In the shelling, the captain was killed, and Simon wounded badly.

Despite being in dreadful shape, Simon managed to crawl from the wreckage up to the deck. He was taken to the medical bay, where four pieces of shrapnel were removed from his body. Simon was not expected to survive the night.

Again he defied the odds and before long returned to active duty. But the ship soon ran aground, and was once again overrun with rats. Simon took to clearing the decks with a renewed sense of purpose. He also visited the infirmary, lifting the spirits of wounded sailors by goofing around and purring while lying next to their heads.

Eventually the *Amethyst* escaped and made her way home. Upon his return, Simon was hailed as a hero by both the British and world press. He was presented with the Dickin Medal, a Blue Cross, and awarded the honorary rank of "Able Seacat." Simon began to receive so much mail that an officer from the *Amethyst* was assigned to answer the thousands of letters.

But like all animals entering Great Britain, Simon was ordered to spend time in quarantine. He obeyed regulations and reported to a facility in Surrey.

While there, Simon became sick with a virus that developed from his war wounds. He passed away on November 28, 1949. The crew of the *Amethyst* and hundreds of others attended his funeral in East London. Simon's gravestone reads:

Simon

SALLY—THE BIG FOURTH AT YALTA

In 1945, World War II was coming to a close. The Allied powers were nearing victory, but many unanswered questions remained about what would happen after Germany surrendered.

On February 4, 1945, the leaders of "The Big Three" Allied countries, Franklin D. Roosevelt from the United States, Winston Churchill of Great Britain, and Soviet premier Joseph Stalin met at Yalta on the Crimean Peninsula. Each was prepared to argue for a postwar arrangement that would specifically benefit his nation. What Roosevelt, Churchill, and Stalin didn't know was that a cat would present the plan that would shape a continent for nearly half a century.

Sally was a Swiss cat with a flair for diplomacy. As a kitten, Sally fought and scrapped her way to the top, but not by biting and scratching in back alleys. She rose through the ranks by gaining consensus, being persuasive, and, if there was no other way to solve an impasse, making deals in back alleys.

When Sally heard what was happening at Yalta, she scurried to the Crimean Peninsula, despite being pregnant. Her goal was to ensure cats still controlled the world, no matter how the Big Three Silly Goofballs divided up the land.

The meeting got off to a bad start. Churchill was mad at Roosevelt. Roosevelt was mad at Stalin. Stalin was mad at everybody. Sally knew what needed to be done. She decided Stalin probably needed the most politicking and started with him.

It didn't take long to figure out that Stalin preferred to be rubbed up against, rather than confronted directly. Sally gave his leg a good working over at every opportunity.

Roosevelt was in a wheelchair most of the time and vulnerable to the charms of a cat on his lap. The U.S. president puffed away on his cigarette holder and turned into a softie.

Churchill was the hardest sell of all. If Sally didn't climb around his neck, he wouldn't give her the time of day. It took a few hours of licking his bald head, but Sally eventually got Churchill's ear.

In spite of Sally's efforts, the Big Three couldn't agree on anything, and worse yet, they hadn't even considered how cats would figure into postwar reconstruction. All parties went grumbling back to their rooms for the night and fell asleep. Sally knew she had to go for broke. It was time for the boldest move in the history of diplomacy.

The Big Three entered the meeting room the next morning and were astonished at what they found. Sally had delivered a litter of kittens upon a giant map of Eastern Europe.

Churchill waddled over and grabbed a kitten off France as fast as he could. Stalin and Roosevelt arrived at Germany and reached simultaneously for the same kitten. Tension filled the air. Would this be what caused the talks to completely break down?

It just so happened that there were two kittens on Germany—one was sleeping on top of the other. Stalin snatched the one that lay most in eastern Germany, while Roosevelt scooped up the western cat.

Once that impasse had been broken, the rest of the map was partitioned very quickly in a similar fashion. Purring kittens dominated every conversation into the evening.

The postwar world was taking shape, and it was guaranteed, cats would influence any major decisions taken by the Big Three powers. Sally had made history.

Sally at Yalta with the Big Three and Kittens

The Scratching Post and Other Postmodern Forms of Control

———— ❖ ————

The insatiable need for control is a defining characteristic of humanity. No other species on the planet is so preoccupied with ensuring their dominance.

Felines have often been caught squarely in the crosshairs of this trait. History is rife with examples of humans attempting to aggressively eliminate "undesirable" cat behaviors, such as scratching.

Early periods saw Romans attempting to stop cats from shredding the backs of their togas. Swatting at the long, braided hair of the Vikings also proved to be a serious point of contention. During this phase, humans resorted mostly to primitive bully tactics, such as smacking and yelling, to try breaking the will of cats.

The postmodern era ushered in new systems to secure obedience. Gone is the classic approach. It has been replaced by a more decentralized model that favors nonviolent deterrents.

Despite undergoing an evolution from base violence to psychological warfare, the goal of humanity remains the same: satisfy a thirst for supremacy.

Nothing they've done has ever worked, of course, but humanity never tires of trying out their bright ideas.

THE SCRATCHING POST

Humans do not recognize furniture scratching as an acceptable method of communicating the desire to jump up on their laps. For reasons as yet undetermined, they have consistently interpreted it as negative and responded passive-aggressively by placing a scratching post in the room.

The look of a scratching post can range from sublime to outrageous. Common features include long shafts covered with rope, elevated seating, and, occasionally, poof balls attached to a metal boingy thing. They are often covered in a material that, to the scratch, makes them feel exactly like the furniture humans sit on.

But a quick examination reveals that no scratching post is intended to support the weight of a human. It becomes obvious that this form of control aims to exploit the probing nature of cats, and their inevitable desire to see what would happen if humans sat on one.

No cat can possibly resist the chance to see this.

Unfortunately, however, the anticipation never ends.

It would appear cats are caught in a vicious paradox, becoming slaves to scratching something that doesn't deliver on its promise. *Theoretically* humans have achieved total control, deciding what furniture to sit on and, by extension, the amount of time per day cats may reside on their laps.

In truth, what occurs is that the scratching post only functions to divert cats for a period of fifteen to forty seconds, just long enough to ensure humans won't try and sit on it. Cats return to scratching furniture, which humans often testily proceed to occupy.

A typical conclusion finds a human with a cat on its lap, pointing to the scratching post, dispensing cursory affection, and then departing. After which, the cycle begins anew.

THE SQUIRT BOTTLE

This method is not completely about control. Use of a squirt bottle also serves to feed humans' morbid fascination with how fast cats can run. A simple, seemingly innocuous, activity like sharpening claws on a rare Persian rug triggers a person's compulsive desire to watch cats take off sprinting.

The squirt bottle/starting gun has proven a highly effective catalyst. It is respected by all cats for an ability to effectively initiate the Skedaddle Reflex. Any cat can be instantly redirected from wherever they're scratching to racing down the hall.

The Scratching Post and Other Postmodern Forms of Control

A squirt bottle is the most controversial device in the postmodern collection. Proper use delivers a psychological attack and low-level physical deterrent simultaneously. No cat can stand the grating "phisst, phisst, phisst" sound, much less being hit with whatever liquid emanates from it.

Fortunately, humans rarely seize the appropriate moment to use a squirt bottle because of a complete inability to remember where it is. Cats typically recognize the frantic squirt bottle hunt, stop scratching, and slink out of the room unscathed.

VINYL NAIL CAPS

The reason for nail caps is as old as humanity itself: jealousy. Humans are no doubt seized with envy upon viewing a cat's claw and immediately need to denigrate what they do not have.

As most cats know, human fingernails are dirty, grimy things that are trimmed by biting when no one is looking or clipped in church. A cat's claw represents something far more elegant and immeasurably cleaner. Claws are also biologically superior, as they do not require paring back.

The caps are small pieces of plastic designed to fit snugly over each of the front claws. Sets come in an array of embarrassing colors such as green, blue, and, worst of all, orange. Cats forced to suffer the indignity of wearing plastic claw covers additionally look trashy.

The bad news is that kittens are a vulnerable group. Many actually accept the caps as an arty fashion statement.

The good news is kittens outgrow that and soon become their own cats, and no cat will be controlled by a human.

Your Attention Span

———— ❧ ————

Humans like to joke about the inconsistent nature of a cat's attention span. What they simply fail to recognize is that when we "spazz," we're just exhibiting a kind of environmental hyperawareness that helps us stay in tune with our surroundings.

Take a look at that sunbeam, for example. It's just the kind of thing that humans ignore every day. Too bad. Isn't sunlight cool? Or, rather, warm. That's what's so cool about it. There was a show on the television once. It was about the stars. Carl Sagan was in it. What do you think of turtlenecks?

It's so weird how TV gets into your house. Why don't we eat turtles? Going fast is awesome. Watch! Vrooooooomm, vroom, zooooooooom! Hey, let's play hidey. Or pretend. No, let's play cat and vet! Who gets to be the cat?

Cats are capable of paying more attention to more things at one time than anybody. In fact, studies show that our average attention span ranges anywhere from two to ten minutes. But you know what's better than paying attention? Belly rubs. Oh, man. The way it makes your tummy feel all tingly? Fantastic. You gotta really trust somebody to let them give you one, though. String beans.

Do you think we'll ever enjoy commercial, affordable spaceflight? Teriyaki chicken and rice is pretty good. Teriyaki. Is that a fish? Does that mean spicy? Cat food is so good. It probably costs like a thousand dollars. Bet you a thousand dollars weighs a thousand pounds. Quarters are shiny. Did you ever spend the whole day chasing one? Another thing humans don't understand is that we cats can pay attention to whatever we want, for as long as we want, but only when we find something interesting. We have the best attention-paying skills, period. You can take that to the bank! You know what else is great? Bicycles.

We're just so lucky that we can look up and see stars and planets and all that stuff at night. It's really fascinating. Maybe Carl Sagan had a cat. Probably named Cosmo! He might have had another cat. The sky is like a bunch of swirly blinky lights. But wait—what about tinfoil? It's hilarious!

In summation, if humans just paid a little more attention themselves, they'd understand that cats are very busy multitaskers. We're constantly looking after things, noticing tiny changes in our environment, and responding to them. Rather than being fundamentally distracted, we're actually extremely attentive. Meanwhile, people are always mucking things up. Forgetting to run to the bank, forgetting to buy litter. If it weren't for all their little day planners, they'd probably forget their own birthdays. When's your birthday? Is it today? You should have a party! Will there be treats? Will there be clowns? No clowns! They're frightening. But balloons are fine. Balloons are great. Everybody loves balloons.

Fat Cats

HEY—WIDE LOAD!

If you're a bit on the jiggly side, it's likely you've been addressed in such a manner. Your person's also probably thrown Captain Waddle-Butt, Eat Machine, and Great Big Fluff Ball of Butter into the mix as well.

People have a habit of making up confusing new names for their chubby kitties. The first time it happens, you may be concerned that your person can't remember your name. What if she has brain worms? Or, worse, what if she thinks you are a different cat? But then it dawns on you that she's just using a bunch of "cutesy" colloquialisms to point out the fact that you are fat! Fatty fat fat!

As if there's something wrong with that. You've got all the awesome things a cat brings to the table, but in a supersized container. Of course you like to eat. Food is delicious. And your person puts it out for you, so eating as much of it as you can just shows an appreciation of her efforts. There certainly is no portion-control function on the bowl that you can see. In fact, she makes three kinds of dry food and two kinds of wet food available daily. Just yesterday she even quite willingly gave you that tub of sour cream to lick clean.

Let's take a look at the facts. A study funded by the Snuggle Institute has proven that moderately sized cats get moderate doses of attention. Cats weighing over thirteen pounds are on the receiving end of an astounding 85 percent more belly rubs than their leaner sisters. Additionally, smooches and squishes are dished out in significantly larger portions to the more ample-sized. In short, big cats are loved in a big way.

So what's with the mixed messages? It's likely your person has fallen victim to the media's obsession with unrealistic body image and almost exclusive focus on willowy kittens.

The good news is that the new digital landscape is finally giving fat cats their due. You don't see pictures of fussy, skinny little tabbies getting forwarded all over the Internet. Who wants to brag about her merely average cat? Everyone's uploading videos and photos of their bountiful beauties kicking back on the couch, watching TV like people. Those cats are famous!

What's important is to always remember that you are perfect just the way you are. And no matter what names your person calls you, know that she loves her big, beautiful cuddly baby more than anything else. Yes she does! Every fuzzy pound of you!

FAT CATS MAKING A DIFFERENCE

Mortimer, an 18½-pound Himalayan of Halifax, Nova Scotia, liked to spend his afternoons gnawing on the mail after it plopped through a slot

in the door. As he tore through the envelope from the gas company each month, he started noticing the heating bills were soaring out of control. Fearing these costs might cut into his treat budget, Mortimer hatched a plan. He got much more needy, sprawling on his person's chest at bedtime and anchoring on her lap during TV time. When his conservation efforts cut the yearly gas bill by almost $500, not only did Mortimer enjoy a bounty of treats, his person upgraded to a premium brand.

Pumpkin Jr., a 17-pound orange tabby from Knoxville, Tennessee, lives with a different kind of person. He is a survivalist who, despite rarely leaving the house, is convinced someone's always trying to poison him. Pumpkin Jr. gladly acts as his food taster, and the arrangement satisfies her hearty appetite just fine. Shrimp's her favorite, so whenever he cooks some up, she acts as though it just might be poisonous till the last bite. And that's a good thing. She's been saving him from a fatal, yet undiagnosed, shellfish allergy for years.

Tidbit, an Aberdeen, Washington, ragamuffin who clocks in at 18¾ pounds under his winter cardigan, is partial to sleeping sprawled out against the back door. In addition to keeping a pesky draft at bay, Tidbit's heft also prevented two break-ins. That got Tidbit a spot on the news. Then a home alarm system company caught wind of it and he wound up with an endorsement deal. Now Tidbit's a local celebrity, and he didn't have to move from his spot for any of it.

Felicia, a 20-pound Russian Blue hailing from St. Louis, Missouri, snuck out of her apartment and got lost in the hall. She was discovered by a neighbor, eighty-seven-year-old Iris Tidlebaum, who took Felicia back to her place to share some ice cream pie. It was Iris's birthday and she was happy to enjoy it with some company. The pie was delicious and Felicia showed her appreciation by snuggling up in Iris's lap. An hour later, a knock at the door revealed Felicia's very relieved person. Iris was very sad to see her go, but in their short time together, fatty little Felicia gave Iris the will to live again.

Fat Cats

Getting Something You Really Need

———— ❧ ————

From chewing cords to throwing up on the most expensive rugs, everything a cat does is for good reason. We don't act out of petty desires or whimsical notions. For example, you aren't on top of the kitchen cabinet because you have a passing fancy to do some light dusting. You are there because you need to experience the kitchen from the most important strategic location in case of a dog attack. On occasion, someone steps in and prevents you from satisfying your needs: your person. You are not without a means of correcting that situation. Here are nine common needs every cat will experience at one time or another, and the best ways to have those needs fulfilled.

The Need	The Obstacle	The Solution
You've had a hard day of napping and playing with some uncooperative string, and you need to be assured that you are special.	Person is staring at a newspaper instead of you.	Park yourself directly between her line of sight and the newspaper, or, better yet, sit directly on it.
You want to spend crucial bonding time with your person.	Person is on the computer, emailing some boy she likes.	Walk on the power strip until her computer shuts down, then jump up for a cuddle.
You want to save some leftover soft food for later.	Your person throws away all uneaten food while "cleaning."	Drag a nearby throw rug to the vicinity and bury it underneath.

The Need	The Obstacle	The Solution
You need some of those delicious chicken treats your owner keeps on hand for special occasions.	Your owner is oblivious to the power of their deliciousness.	Pretend it's your birthday.
Your primal urge to hunt is welling up inside.	You knocked your last mousie under the closet door.	Station yourself in front of the door, reaching under it as far as you can. Look pathetically at your person and meow. As soon as she fishes it out, knock it back under there.
That pill in the person's hand must not go down your throat.	Your person is holding you down while popping your mouth open to make you swallow it.	Move your head back and forth, knock her hands away with your paws, or force the pill out of the side of your mouth with your tongue. If there are two people in on the pill taking, swallow it as fast as possible and get it over with.
It's time for your favorite show, *Amazing Buzzing Insect.*	The blinds are drawn.	Climb under the blinds or bat at them until your person comes and opens them for you.
You need to get some sleep.	It's 2:00 a.m. and the party guests won't leave.	Wander into the middle of the action and throw up on the floor. Watch the guests scatter.
You need to send your person a reminder that it's all about you.	A strange human is taking up all your person's time.	Play up to the new human. Become your person's rival for his affections.

Extrasensory Pussycats

Have you ever been absolutely certain your person was heading home, even though it was only noon and she should still be at work? You staked out your spot in the window, like it was her regular time to arrive home, and then—there she was, walking up the driveway, just like that!

But how did you know?

If she'd been sitting around the house, counting embezzlement money, you probably had a good sense she was on her way to getting canned. If not, it was likely a premonition borne out of certain special abilities you possess. Now, we're not talking about your everyday special abilities, like being able to zero in on your new toy in a sea of shopping bags. These are *extra*-special abilities—and they are *mental*.

But before you break out the crystal ball and set up a feline psychic hotline, know that these gifts are pretty common in cats, though they tend to be seen more frequently in the left-pawed among us. So if you're a righty, go back to sleep. You're probably just regular.

Humans who have studied our uncanny talents often explain them away as reactions to smells, sounds, or changes in the magnetic field. But that's just a bunch of lazy pseudoscience.

The reality is that in addition to our already highly evolved brains, many of us have a high-wattage titanium-alloy antenna hidden deep within our tails. This instrument transmits signals to specific parts of the brain and unlocks certain mysterious features. Combined, they unleash the awesome powers of feline extrasensory perception!

So, you may be wondering, if your brain-tail combo is so awesome, how come it's only keeping track of your person's humdrum schedule? Well, that's its most basic function, sort of like a built-in BlackBerry. There are a whole lot more cool bells and whistles at your disposal.

Finding Your Way Home: When a cat travels a long distance to get back to her person, the antenna taps into the GPS function of the temporal lobe (and, unlike human GPS systems, ours know where the detours are). A Persian mix named Sugar pushed the limits of this feature in the granddaddy journey of them all. Her family moved from California to Oklahoma, but sadly left her behind with friends because a hip deformity made it difficult for her to travel. After a few weeks, Sugar ran away from the friend's place and fourteen months later showed up on her family's doorstep in Oklahoma—1,500 miles from her original home, to a place she'd never been before, bum hip and all! Sugar's GPS broke after that. Now she's stuck in Oklahoma, but that's okay, because she's home now.

Human Illness: You can always tell when your person is feeling under the weather. That's because your tail antenna is equipped to act as a CAT scan, sending its readings to the brain for analysis. Sometimes this ability can even save a life. For instance, Tee-Cee, a no-nonsense tuxedo cat from England, regularly monitors his person's vitals for the signs of an impending seizure. When Tee-Cee picks up signals that one is imminent, he gets right up in his person's face and stares at him real good. Any time he starts doing that, his person's family is ready to call for medical attention if needed. Because of his CAT scanner skills, Tee-Cee was even named 2006 Rescue Cat of the Year!

The Final Hours: Even when very far apart, some cats know the moment their people pass away, and become visibly distressed. Other cats have the ability to recognize the onset of death in humans that aren't even theirs. The most famous cat to put this to use is Oscar, unfortu-nately dubbed "the death cat," but who actually should be known as "the comfort cat."

Oscar resides at a Providence, Rhode Island, nursing home and received international media attention after the facility's staff noticed he'd curl up with patients several hours before they passed away. After Oscar had a streak of correct predictions, doctors decided to start notifying family members when he snuggled up with their loved one. This gave the families time to say goodbye, and if they couldn't make it, Oscar was still there with the patients at the end. For his compassion, Oscar was presented with an award and has a plaque hanging at the facility in his honor.

Earthquakes: Because of the antenna's seismometer function, cats know when to scram before an earthquake hits. Historians have noted that in 373 B.C., cats fled the Greek city of Helice days before it was leveled by an earthquake (some other animals were also said to have fled, undoubtedly taking their cue from in-the-know cats). Chinese humans have long been aware of the ability cats have to predict quakes. In 1975, when cats started going haywire in the city of Haicheng, the place was evacuated. Several days later, a devastating earthquake hit. Those worked-up cats got the credit for saving thousands of human lives.

Every tail antenna comes with its own special custom features, so keep testing yours out to see what else it can do. However, it's important not to abuse your special abilities or allow anyone to take advantage of them. So if you discover a lottery predictor tucked away in there, we suggest keeping it to yourself. Otherwise your toys will be limited to white balls with numbers written on them from here on out.

Booby-Trapping the Home

One day you're just excavating the gardenia and chewing on cords behind the TV, like usual. The next, everything's a horrifying mess of tinfoil and double-sided tape. What gives? Your person has set up what are known as "booby traps." She's trying to keep you out of certain places, but sent her flunky foil and icky double-sided tape to do the dirty work.

Has it ever occurred to her that there are areas *you'd* prefer to have all to yourself? Obviously not, or she wouldn't be lying on the couch all the time.

But there's nothing stopping you from setting up booby traps of your own.

STAIR TOYS

Nothing's worse than being sprawled out on your favorite stair, dreaming of a piping hot chipmunk tart, and getting the boot because someone's trying to carry a hot water heater down to the basement. Don't they know Tuesdays are no good for deliveries? To keep your person and her appliance-toting associates off the stairs, we recommend leaving strategically placed balls, mousies, and other toys in locations where they are sure to be stepped on or tripped over. Over time, your person should learn to avoid the area.

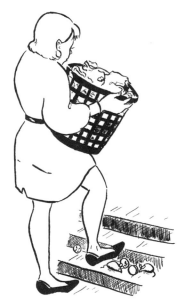

HELLO HAIRBALL!

Every well-groomed cat needs to hack up a hairball on occasion, so why not leave it in a key location to get a point across? Hairballs are versatile booby traps that can be used in a wide array of situations, and even on humans other than your person. When you want to dissuade a certain human from keeping

company with your person, a hairball booby trap does the perfect trick. Just hack one up in his shoe. Nothing says "stay out of my house" quite like a leather loafer filled with your moist regurgitated fur. Consistently apply this technique over time and you will start seeing considerably less of this unsavory character.

BATHTUB BOTTLE CAP

When you get all pie-eyed and nutso, the bathtub is one of the best places to scramble around like a maniac. Except if your person was in there first. Then it's all wet and nasty. Well, there's a way to curb her inconsiderate behavior while also having a blast. Late at night, while she's sound asleep, haul your favorite bottle cap into the tub and bat it around in the dark for hours of fun. When you're done, leave it upside down, right near the center. Come morning when your bleary-eyed person hops in for her shower, she should step right on your booby trap. Even if she doesn't, it may still manage to clog the drain.

INDOOR WATERFALL

Here's a good tactic to use if your water dish is not being refreshed as often as you like. It's difficult to pull off solo, as it involves a hoist, winch, and an intricate series of pulleys, so if there are other cats in the house to recruit, or if there's a big, gullible dog you might finally put to some good use, seek them out.

Locate a heavily trafficked door that is left slightly ajar and drag the dirty drinking bowl toward it. Now without spilling, hoist the bowl up and balance it cautiously on the top of that door. When your person pushes it open, the filthy water, filled with chunks of bloated dry food, litter bits, and dead insects, will come crashing down on her head. Guess who's getting one of those fancy, constantly refreshing drinking fountains now?

In Defense of Your Discriminating Palate

———————— ❧ ————————

W e'll be the first to admit that we're highly opinionated around the food bowl. Cats like to take care of themselves, and are mindful of what they put into their bodies. We firmly believe that all vittles should be highly delectable.

Yet unsavory meals are served to cats every day, in food bowls all across the country. Hearty giblets with gravy may sound like an appealing entrée, if served precisely at feline body temperature, on a spotless plate, accompanied by a bowl of fresh springwater. But if even one element is missing, you may as well eat a bowl of rocks that resemble hearty giblets with gravy, because that is what your dinner will taste like.

Are we finicky? No. But we do know what we like. We also know what we don't like, and we're not afraid to turn our noses up at a sub-par meal.

It's no surprise that this behavior boggles your person's mind. This is the same woman who throws perfectly good gizzards in the trash. Clearly, good taste is not her territory. She may never understand your special likes and dislikes, but perhaps by arming yourself with the following information, you can teach her how your so-called fussiness is really just a function of the unique cat anatomy—namely, your amazing nose and tongue.

A NOSE FOR FLAVOR

If the complaint against our species was possession of a keen and excellent sense of smell, we would plead guilty as charged. As with humans, cats' noses work in conjunction with their taste buds. Not surprisingly, though, the cat's nose is far superior to the human's, and is thus used to greater effect. We use smell to help us detect extremely minute changes in food, which is how we know if prey is diseased, or if our wet food's spoiled. It's also how we know that the fisherman who caught the shrimp we're refusing recently switched soaps. No offense, we just don't find the lingering scent of Dial very pleasing on the whiskers.

Our insistence on maximum freshness is a holdover characteristic from the days when we caught and killed everything we ate. Nowadays, the only thing most of us catch at mealtime is flak for being fusspots, but we still put a premium on eating food at its best. Our "secret weapon" for evaluating freshness and flavor is called the Jacobson's organ. It's located in the roof of the mouth and is connected to the nasal passages. By opening our mouths and sneering, we can actually smell and taste an odor at the same time. This action is called the Flehmen response. Its purpose is to capture the odor on the tongue, and send it to the Jacobson's organ for analysis.

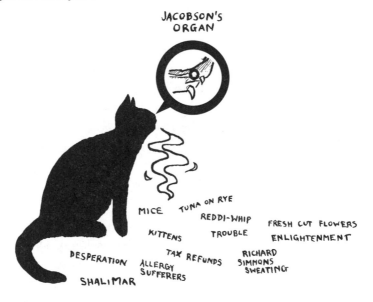

JACOBSON'S
ORGAN

MICE TUNA ON RYE
REDDI-WHIP
KITTENS TROUBLE FRESH CUT FLOWERS
ENLIGHTENMENT
DESPERATION TAX REFUNDS RICHARD
ALLERGY SIMMONS
SUFFERERS SWEATING
SHALIMAR

In Defense of Your Discriminating Palate

THE TOOLS OF THE TRADE

Once we've smelled a chicken drumstick and it's passed muster, we might actually want to eat it. Luckily, our rough, barbed tongues are up for the job. With two sets of taste buds, we're able to experience a wide array of delicate flavors and register all kinds of textures and shapes. The one thing we can't really do is detect sweets. That doesn't mean we don't eat marshmallows, or want to eat marshmallows. It just means we can't taste marshmallows.

Another cool thing about our tongues is the small, bulbous papillae that cover them. We use these tiny hook-shaped bits to lick every last morsel of meat clean off the bone.

We can also shape our tongues into very efficient spoons, in order to quickly lap up tasty fresh cream or water. It's nature's answer to the spork.

If after this brief lesson you still find yourself accused of being an overly persnickety pussycat, we suggest you cut out the following list and tape it to the refrigerator door. While by no means exhaustive, it should clear up any lingering doubts regarding what you should be fed.

WHAT WE WILL NOT EAT

What is in the bowl
Anything purchased in bulk
The brand of cat food on sale this week
Whopper Jr.
Expensive organic supposedly healthy cat treats

WHAT WE'LL EAT WHEN WE FEEL LIKE IT

Creamed corn
Unattended raviolis
Quarter Pounder with Cheese
The occasional piece of plastic wrap
Expensive organic supposedly healthy cat treats

WHAT'S WRONG WITH OUR FOOD TODAY?

Too salty
Not salty enough
Only mildly delicious
Doesn't look right
Incorrect pH balance
Several degrees too warm

It really couldn't be much simpler than that.

Your First Kitty Condo—Making the Leap

Home ownership is a dream of many cats. It's also a pretty big, life-changing decision and not something to take lightly. As a first-time house hunter, carefully consider your needs and priorities while surveying the condo market. It will probably be your home for a long time. Don't get stuck living out your golden years on a mangy, secondhand perch by the litter box.

The first hurdle is securing an agent. This is tough, as the kitty condo real estate profession isn't a particularly competitive field. In fact, your person is the only agent practicing in your area. Insist she put on a tan blazer so this part of your relationship can maintain a detached air of professionalism.

As your agent will surely say, it's all about location, location, location! Are you a sneaky, private cat looking to put down stakes in a secluded nook? Maybe you're hoping for prime window-front property overlooking the bird feeder. Select a few favored areas and start spending time in them during different hours of the day. The south side of the guest room might seem like the ideal sun-splashed locale, but the ceiling above could get drippy when it rains. Also, don't find out after it's too late that you're living next to the nightly meet-up spot for an opossum jamboree.

Within each neighborhood you'll find an array of choices for every lifestyle and budget. You might be satisfied with a simple bed atop a sisal-rope-covered pole; or you may crave variety and room to spread out. Whatever it is, be sure to make a decision based on what's right for you. Just because that snooty Manx next door slinks around on a five-tiered unit custom-crafted to look like a Japanese pagoda doesn't mean you need the same. Spending all your free time trying to maintain a big, empty, rug-covered castle just because you want to outdo your neighbor is no way to live.

At this point your agent will start showing what's currently on the market. If you see something you like, don't rush into the deal. Always do a proper inspection before closing. A bunch of dangling ropes may seem like a great feature until you crash to the hardwood floor after one of the ropes yanks free under your weight.

Your agent will likely show you several models similar to these:

This shag duplex makes a cozy starter home.
Embarrassing stains need not be a problem as the custom-carpet option allows you to choose the color most resembling your favorite shade of food!

Your First Kitty Condo—Making the Leap

A playground of your own!

You want to be on there? How about under here? Oh, there's a neat spot. Then you can shimmy down the pole and jump in there! With enough room to entertain, you can finally invite over all those cool cats who hang out in the alley.

Paradise!

Crank up the Don Ho, scramble up the trunk, and relax in your very own faux coconut. Even if you live in Buffalo, every day can be a tropical dream with this beauty!

After checking out all the options with your agent, you might just realize that what you're looking for could actually be right where you are. But first your person will need to lose that silly tan blazer and get herself a tool belt.

Instead of a whole new abode, renovating your person's home to meet your needs may be the way to go. There is limitless potential. With built-in shelves, wall-mounted perches, and suspended hammocks, it's possible to transform an entire room into a magical Kitty Land!

After all, what does your person really need an office for, anyway? That space couldn't possibly be put to any better use than as your home sweet home!

The Pros and Cons of Being Sullen

Sometimes, cats are just in a bad mood. We wake up and just don't have it in us to frolic, munch, or even nap. No, we are fussy, crabby, even cantankerous, and there's no end in sight for such a mood. The good thing is that we don't necessarily have to raise our spirits. Sometimes, the best thing one can do when feeling dour is to ride it out. Here are some factors to weigh when you are thinking about whether or not to wallow in a bad mood.

PROS

- You get a wide berth from your person and other animals in the house.
- There's finally a justification for swatting at anything or anyone that crosses your path.
- Food tastes better when eaten with attitude.
- Sitting sourly in one place allows your overworked muscles to relax.
- Humans act like you are sick instead of cross, which can result in treats.
- You can work on your screenplay about a cat who is the president.
- By being completely still for a long period of time, a mouse may pass in front of you so that you can snatch it.
- Being crabby settles the stomach.
- Periods of sullen inactivity slow the heart and help you live a little longer.
- It's as good a reason as any to sit still and glower for hours on end.
- You can mentally re-rank your favorite toys.
- By assuming the sullen posture, you create a natural arch, one of the strongest of structural forms.

- It's good for your fur.
- You can exercise your rarely used lower vocal range when you growl at everything.
- Catch up on your bristling.
- Calibrate your ears by moving them toward every little sound without moving the rest of your body.
- Even though everything is always about you, everything is even more about you.
- It makes your happier moods seem all the better when contrasted with your sullenness.
- It transitions nicely into a refreshing nap.
- You can spy on everyone in the house and take notes for later.
- Being sullen enables you to tap into your primal jungle cat.
- You can do an inventory of your body and make sure that all your parts are in place.
- It helps you to memorize every aspect of the room, which makes for a great party trick later.
- Your tail can get a good workout by whipping it around like a maniac.
- Someone might come by and cheer you up against your better judgment by petting you.
- After a while, you will forget what made you sullen in the first place.
- If you stare hard and sullenly enough, you can see through walls.

CONS

- None come to mind.

Outsmarting Your Toys

Toys are a bit of an enigma. They simultaneously bug and beckon, and always manage to take you away at inopportune times from stuff you need to do. Think about it. Or maybe you can't because a toy is in your face, distracting you, right now. That's kind of the point. Playing with a toy that your person puts in front of you is unavoidable. You can, however, outsmart your toy so it stops bugging you. That way you'll be able to get back to more important tasks much faster.

TUNNELS

Even though it isn't exactly a toy, a tunnel has the toylike capacity to trick you into wasting tons of time. You can almost hear it saying, "Here kitty, kitty, kitty! Come on in! I promise you can leave any time you want!" Then you realize the second you enter that it's a trap. Yes, the exit is right in front of you, and also right behind you, but what if the second you leave something awesome happens in the tunnel? It's not worth it to risk missing something awesome!

The tunnel believes it is smarter than you because it forces you to be inside of it in order to see what's going on . . . inside of it. To turn the tables on a terrible tunnel, rip it wide open.

Enter one of the openings of the tunnel just like you normally would. Don't let on you have any semblance of a plan. Then when you reach the midpoint, go nuts. Spazz out with your tail out. Swing your claws so fast that it looks like you have eight arms. Become a true octopussy.

Soon, your wild slashes will create a new opening in the tunnel and you'll be able to escape the very belly of the beast. That gaping hole will allow you to see what's going on inside the tunnel without having to physically enter, and it will make the toy think twice about tempting you into its bamboozling bowels the next time.

DANGLERS

Sometimes these bouncy sticks have a bunch of feathers at the end, sometimes there's just a piece of cardboard, but either way, the goal is the same: flip through the air, trying to rip the thing off the stick and get on with your day. Taking out one of these infuriating busybodies is normally very exhausting. They act as if they want to talk to you by getting really close, but then dart away, but then come back, but then zip away, but then hit you on the head. After a seemingly endless swatting session, you can usually get a dangler to sit still, but by then you're too worn out to pick up the quilt-destruction project where you left off before the dangler arrived. Fortunately, there is a way to get the same result in half the time using far less effort.

When a dangler taps you on the face for the first time, just walk away. The method seems a little backward, but within seconds the dangler will stop moving—usually around the same time your human leaves the room. Then, just jet back in and destroy whatever it is that's on the end of that stick! If you leave the room and come back a few minutes later to find your person is still playing with the dangler by herself, there might be something wrong with her. Keep an eye on the situation.

TREAT BALLS

Is there anything sweeter than the taste of victory over a toy? Yes. The taste of a chicken 'n' liver treat extracted from the inside of a toy. Unfortunately, treat balls are real teases. They mock you by keeping their delicious insides locked up and inaccessible. Removing a treat from the center of one of these confounded plastic or plush contraptions can take hours of earnest pawing and nibbling. With a little bit of ingenuity, however, you can be munching on toy innards in short order.

Don't be fooled if the ball has a hard shell. It's a weakling on the inside. To get to the good stuff fast, smack it off the edge of someplace really high up, like the top of a staircase or a balcony, then run down to feast on its remains. Make sure to get to the shattered toy before any children or squirrels have a chance to steal your treat.

Plush toys don't let go of treats as easily as their plastic counterparts. A thirty-foot drop from a second-floor window only seems to make the toy more intent on keeping a treat for itself and wasting your valuable time in the process. However, with a little help from technology, specifically blending technology, you can get at the treat with virtually no labor. When your person isn't around, leap up on the kitchen counter with your toy in mouth. Then, drop it into a blender or food processor, secure the top, and smack whatever setting you see fit. We suggest FRAPPE, if that is an option. It produces a delightful, thick, and refreshing stuffing-and-kibble blend.

LASER POINTER TOYS

Laser pointers are a new breed of toy that many cats are still confounded by. Obviously the laser dot is outsmarted when it is covered up, but that little red bugger is a cunning creature. It seems no matter how fast you pounce, it always manages to get on top of your paw first. The ordeal can take hours and the only method cats have come up with to beat a laser pointer is to smack the light until it gradually fades out. There's a faster way. The next time that obnoxious dot appears, go to your person's makeup drawer and take out her compact mirror. It's a little-known fact that mirrors are the natural enemies of lasers. Wait until the dot is on the floor and then slide the mirror under it. Just as fast as it hits the floor, the laser will dart away, leaving you to celebrate by licking the face of your person, who, for some reason, is shielding her eyes and yelling something about going blind.

Planning Your Next Vacation

When your person packs her bags and leaves for a while, why not take a holiday yourself and recharge?

VISIT A NATURAL WONDER

An awe-inspiring scene of nature's splendor is a must on any itinerary. Even the most jaded soul can be invigorated by such a sight. Fortunately, all cats have such a place to enjoy and it's as close as the nearest bathroom.

Experiencing this monument while on vacation is a special

treat. Start by climbing up on the edge. Then reach over with your paw and push the lever.

Take a look down for a glimpse of nature's awesome

power! Be careful not to fall in, though. You'll be a goner. Nature can be very moving but also sometimes cruel and unforgiving.

Feel free to stay for a while. The scene is so impressive that some cats watch it four or five thousand times!

STRETCH OUT ON A BEACH

We all enjoy a nice sunbathing session from time to time, but not many of us have been to the beach.

If your person enjoys crafts, scan all the windows in the house for a dream catcher or stained-glass butterfly. Should you find either thing, check for a sand sculpture on the windowsill below. There's a decent chance it's there.

If so, you're in luck, because that means there's also a beach nearby. Carefully tip the thing over. Carefully! You don't want to spill beach into the homemade wicker basket under the window. Sitting in a makeshift magazine rack full of sand is not the same as being at the beach.

Once all the sand is spread out, it's time to lie down and soak up those rays. Sand warms up better than carpet. As always, make sure to drink plenty of water and protect your nose with a high-SPF sunscreen if sunbathing for long periods.

HAVING FANCY MEALS

Good food is a big part of any vacation. So make sure you get it, even if that means sucking up to the waitstaff a little.

When your person leaves, somebody else will take her food-serving shifts. Getting to know a new server and greasing the wheels a bit can ensure fantastic meals for the duration of your vacation.

Fill-in servers appreciate being well treated. Often they're short on experience and a little nervous about attending

to your needs. If you show them kindness and respect, they'll usually return the favor by bringing dishes that are not on the regular menu.

Remember to always tip generously. Your fill-in server doesn't make much and depends on gratuities to keep doing the job.

CATCH UP ON YOUR READING

Vacation isn't just about sightseeing and enjoying creature comforts. Consider kicking back with a book.

If you've got a beach, that's a perfect place; otherwise, just sprawl out anywhere comfortable and lose yourself in words. An afternoon with a good book might be what rekindles your love of reading!

SIGHTS OFF THE BEATEN PATH

There may come a time when you want to get away from the touristy stuff and venture off the beaten path. That's when you should check out some place with local flavor.

Here's just such a destination, and it's rarely advertised. To get there you need to locate a magic door, which is usually found in the ceiling of a bedroom closet.

To pass through the magic door, climb up the clothes and stand on the bar they hang on. When ready, jump up and grab the rope to the magic door. After it opens, just walk up the stairs to gain admission.

Welcome to a whole new area to explore and investigate. It can be oppressively hot during summer and bitterly cold in the winter, so we advise an autumn visit if at all possible.

This out-of-the-way spot is rich in local history. Boxes of old papers, photographs, and clothes abound, and crowds are light. About the only time humans visit here and really look around is when desperately trying to find a birth certificate. On your trip, there certainly won't be a line to view running shorts from 1982, or a faked old-timey picture of the whole family sporting western wear and firearms.

Sometimes these places have old stuff that's valuable, and humans often don't even know about it. Things like a Stradivarius violin worth U.S. $3,544,000 at auction, or a very fine copy of Action Comics number one featuring the debut of Superman, valued at $1,560,000. If you come across anything like that, take it as a souvenir for your person. She'll really appreciate it.

If you hang around long enough, some exotic local fauna might make an appearance. A bat sighting at the end of an attic visit can leave you with an irre-

placeable vacation memory. Just make sure to keep your distance. They don't like tourists.

After the day is done, head back home and enjoy all the wild nightlife that normally gets you chased into the basement by your person. Really tear it up. After all, she's gone and you're on vacation!

The Nine Lives of Mr. Champ

———————— 🐾 ————————

Most of us like to get into a bit of trouble every now and then. What's a cut here or a scrape there if it's all in the name of good, clean cat fun?

Some of the more adventurous kitties among us even use up a life or two in the course of a year. But you'd have to be a VERY bold pussycat to use up eight of your nine lives in as many days.

In fact, in all of feline history, there is only one kitty rumored to have achieved this incredible feat. He was the legendary Mr. Champ, a fun-loving, tortoiseshell mix with a devil-may-care attitude who hailed from the city of Las Vegas, Nevada.

So large was his legend that many cat historians doubted his very existence. They felt strongly that no one cat could get into so much trouble so quickly, and believed him to be a sort of mythical composite cat, like the human King Arthur, or the Emperor Charlemagne. Others felt there was substantial evidence to suggest that Mr. Champ was in fact an actual cat who lived and was active in the western United States during the twenty-first century. Their best estimates place him in the Las Vegas area sometime between 1980 and 2004.

The controversy came to a head on June 17, 2006, when a diary surfaced at a Reno rummage sale. The diary detailed the exploits of one very daring cat who called himself Mr. Champ and lived his lives at an astounding pace. This discovery literally turned the cat world upside down. If Mr. Champ were real—if a cat that brave had also been a house cat—what would it mean for domestic cats, and domestic catkind? Indeed, cat philosophers continue to consider the question to this day.

Though the jury is still out on whether the diary is a fake, most cats believe it is authentic, and many take it to be incontrovertible proof of

Mr. Champ's glorious existence. If true, one cannot help but wonder where he is now, and what he is doing.

The following is an excerpt from this fearless kittycat's diary:

May 12
Dear Diary:

You'll never believe what happened today. I was sitting out in front of our building, sniffing hello to the day, when I looked up and spotted a jogger tying her shoe in the street. She had headphones on, and didn't notice a big camper heading right toward her. He was honking the horn, but she didn't seem to hear it. If she didn't move fast, she was going to get hit!

I couldn't let that happen. I had to do something. I darted out after her, meowing and hissing to get her attention. She saw me and I pointed my paw at the camper. She moved out of the way just in the nick of time, and I felt like I was really living up to my name. I felt like a real champ. I felt like a hero!

Then I felt kind of woozy, like a kitty who just got clipped by a Winnebago.

May 13
Dear Diary:

I spent most of yesterday cuddling and recuperating. Everyone was so nice to me after the accident. Turns out the Winnebago driver could see the jogger all along—he just couldn't see me. He took me straight to the vet, who pronounced me one lucky, healthy kitty, and he sent us a pretty bouquet of lilies. The jogger sent a big bag of treats over, and my person, Mary, has been extra nice to me.

I have to admit, it was kind of fun flying through the air after I got hit. I felt like I was starring in a kitty kung-fu movie. Hey—maybe I could be a stunt-cat!

Of course Mary doesn't want me doing any more stunts, or saving any more lives. She's mad I was even outside. *Who am I gonna save in the house, a load of laundry? Anyway, she isn't treating me like a hero. She's treating me like a baby. In fact, she's making me stay inside all day today.*

Man, these lilies smell great. And they're so pretty! I wonder how they taste?

May 14

I learned a valuable lesson yesterday. No snack is worth a trip to the emergency room. Anyway, how was I supposed to know lilies would make me feel all oogy? You would think that florists would put a kitty skull and crossbones on them or something. The good news is, I'm feeling much better already. And it's a beautiful day! Mary's opened all the windows up and the place is full of fresh air. It's also full of horseflies. I've been playing with one all morning. I named him Ricardo. We live on the 4th floor and I keep wondering, how does a little pest like that get all the way up here?

However he did it, Ricardo obviously doesn't know how to get out. He's just buzzing around like a real dummy. I'm tired of having him here. He can go buzz off somewhere else and drive some other cat crazy!

Well, I'll show him. I'm gonna chase that stupid fly right over to the window! I'm gonna head him off by the window! I'm gonna follow him right out the—

Uh-oh.

May 15

It's official—four stories is now my all-time height record for falling out of a window. Mary was pretty shook up yesterday after I fell. She was surprised to see that I was okay. I wasn't surprised. I always land on my feet! Except for that one time with the cactus plants.

Anyway, Mary's so nervous, she put a guard up on the ledge today, which is really gonna mess with my window-viewing time. But I guess it'll keep me from taking another dive.

I'm pretty bored, though. Maybe I should go take a closer look at those three little holes in the wall. It's funny, but I've never understood how those work. I know Mary puts a special kind of string inside of it, like the one attached to the hair dryer, and it makes the hair dryer purr.

I really want to know how this works. Hey—maybe if I put my paw in there the way she puts the string in there, I'll purr, too!!! I'll do a science experiment!!

Note to self: In the future, leave science to the professionals.

May 16

Another beautiful day. I thought I would sneak outside and see what was going on in the neighborhood. Plus, with all the trouble I've been getting into in the house lately, I'm probably better off out there.

I'm sitting there, sunning myself on the sidewalk and cleaning my fur, when I hear a really big CRASSHH!!! coming from back by the garbage cans. I go around to investigate, and what do I find? A raccoon! Wow! I've never seen one before, but if I remember from my reading, they're supposed to be very friendly toward cats. I think he wants to play!

May 17
    Dear Diary:

I was grossly misinformed about raccoons.

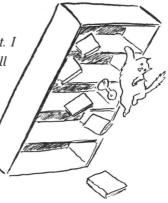

    Anyway, I think I put up a pretty good fight. I got a couple of rabies shots, and the vet said it will only be about two weeks before my whiskers grow back. In the meantime, maybe I'll catch up on my gossip mags. I just love hearing about what celebrity cats are getting into! Mary keeps all the magazines on the top shelf of her bookcase, but I think I can reach them. I just have to climb onto the couch . . . then the ledge . . . then the first shelf . . . and then, reach . . .

May 18

I guess I don't know my own strength. Anyway, I spent about 45 minutes under there before anybody found me. It was okay, though. I played kitty fort. Also, I was buried under a copy of Old Possum's Book of Practical Cats, *and I have concluded that T. S. Eliot probably never met a real cat in his entire life.*

May 19
    Dear Diary:

The rumors are true. I got stuck in the heating duct. Again. And I do not want to discuss it.

May 20

Finally! The end of the week. I managed to get myself into some real predicaments, but I feel great. I'm just a little tired. All I really want to do is curl up and take a nap in a nice, quiet, snuggly, warm dark place.

Like here! This place looks perfect!

Whhhhhyyyyy is evverrytthhhing spiiningnignignggg?

May 21

Dear Diary:

You know, I had some time to think when I was being tumble-dried. A kitty may have nine lives, but he's got to spend each one like it's the only one he's got. Mischief is great, but all these close calls have helped me figure out how I want to spend the rest of my lives.

It may not be a big adventure, but it's the best feeling I know.

ACKNOWLEDGMENTS

Some thank-yous are in order:

ACTION 5: John Huston, Baly Cooley, Mike Loew, Victoria Skurnick, Daniel Greenberg, Elizabeth Fisher, Bruce Tracy, Patty Park, Ryan Doherty, and Rob Pesce.

ANITA: Mum Maria and Pops David Serwacki, Pupka, Julianne Serwacki, Joan and Bob McDonald, the Camacho family, the Rose family, Kathy Kobler, and my stable of feline goons.

CHRIS: Heather Sabin, Dale and Susan Pauls, Todd, Heather, Carter and Jackson Pauls, Dorothy Pauls, Doug Smith and entire Smith Family, Matt Solomon, John and Jim Roach, *The Onion,* and all my friends at the Village Bar.

JANET: Barbara, Harold, and Matthew Ginsburg; my dad, Roy; Camille Rose Garcia, Cheryl Benson, Dennis Messner, Traci Gallagher, Eileen Pierce, Q-Tip, and my supportive friends and family the world over.

JOE: My family (especially Violet, because her brother got a clandestine heads-up in the last book), Nick Gallo, *The Onion,* Smartie, and Tiny. Oh, and that crybaby Bill Jackson.

SCOTT: Beryl and Leigh Sherman, the late Karl Weintraub, the Second City, *The Onion,* David Miner, Greg Walter, Bryan Saunders, Chidozie Ugwumba, Andy Elkin, Dianne McGunigle, and Ella.

ACTION 5 is a comedy-writing collective based in New York and Wisconsin. Their previous book, *The Dangerous Book for Dogs,* is available from Villard.

www.action5.com

Individually, they are:

JOE GARDEN is the features editor of *The Onion.* He has portrayed an angry file cabinet on a late-night cartoon, a morgue assistant on a straight-to-DVD film, and, with his wife, Anita Serwacki, has written for the Emmy-winning cartoon *WordGirl.* He has one cat, Smartie, who is finally earning her keep, and had another cat, Tiny, whom he misses dearly.

JANET GINSBURG has worked as a field producer on *The Daily Show with Jon Stewart* and is a former staff writer for *The Onion.* She has also written or produced programs for the Discovery, Sci-Fi, and E! Entertainment channels, and her work has appeared in publications such as *Vibe, Blender,* and the *LA Weekly.* She was good friends with a cat named Q-Tip. She lives in Brooklyn.

CHRIS PAULS is a contributing writer to *The Onion* and does other stuff, too. He lives in Middleton, Wisconsin, with his wife and three cats, Freddie, Albert, and BB King.

ANITA SERWACKI is a contributing writer for *The Onion* and has written for the PBS animated series *WordGirl.* She was music supervisor on the documentary *The Kid Stays in the Picture* and has been a DJ in N.Y.C. for many years, mostly on the burlesque circuit. Growing up, her family had a cat named Samantha, who taught herself to use the toilet, which was weird. After just one week Samantha stopped using the toilet and never did it again, which was weirder. She currently lives in Brooklyn with her husband, Joe Garden, and *her* cats Bacon and Pokey. Tiny RIP.

SCOTT SHERMAN is a staff writer for *Important Things with Demetri Martin* on Comedy Central. He is a former contributing writer for *The Onion* and the Onion News Network, and has also written for *The New York Times Magazine,* Spike TV, and A&E. He lives in New York City.

ABOUT THE ILLUSTRATOR

EMILY FLAKE is an illustrator, cartoonist, and author. She is the creator of the cartoon strip *Lulu Eightball,* which runs in altweeklies across the country, as well as the author of the Prism Award–winning book *These Things Ain't Gonna Smoke Themselves.* She lives in Brooklyn. Look up her work at eflakeagogo.com.

ABOUT THE TYPE

This book is set in Cheltenham, a typeface originally conceived as a book type by Bertram Goodhue, a considerable American architect. As Alexander Lawson wrote in his *Anatomy of a Typeface,* "In the post–World War II era, when its use declined, it became the subject of numerous articles in printing-trade periodicals, most expressing divided opinions on its pedigree as a good letter form or its usefulness as a typeface." What better face to use than one that brings up discussions of pedigree? Whether for thoroughbreds or felines, Chelt does the job.